CHAMBERS

Spell Well!

CHAMBERS

Spell Well!

Compiled by
E. M. Kirkpatrick
and C. M. Schwarz

Chambers

ISBN 0 550 11821 7 (*hardback*)
     0 550 71312 3 (*limp*)

Printed in Great Britain
at the University Press, Cambridge

Preface

All but the most brilliant of spellers — and few people claim to be in that class — have to check the spelling of certain words from time to time. Some of us have a few blind spots, such as *correspondence*, which we can never remember how to spell. Others — although otherwise intelligent and educated! — are poor spellers generally.

Of course ordinary dictionaries can be used to check the spelling of words but that involves sifting through information which is not at that moment required. Chambers *Spell Well!* has been designed for ease of reference so that people can find quickly and easily the words which they have difficulty in spelling.

It provides in a simple, easy-to-follow, form the common words that are likely to cause spelling problems. We have deliberately not included words such as *aardvark* which the man in the street is unlikely to want to use. If people do require help with spelling such words they will find them in one of our wide range of dictionaries.

About this guide

The words in Chambers *Spell Well!* are clearly listed in alphabetical order.

Those parts of speech which are liable to cause spelling problems are listed under the relevant word, e.g.:

Adverbs

basic	public	wilful
adv basically	*adv* publicly	*adv* wilfully

Plurals

factory	monkey	potato
pl factories	*pl* monkeys	*pl* potatoes
piano	crisis	thief
pl pianos	*pl* crises	*pl* thieves

Where more than one plural is allowable both have been given, e.g.

referendum	banjo
pl referenda, referendums	*pl* banjos, banjoes

Parts of verbs

gallop	refer	swim	light
galloped	referred	swam	lit, lighted
galloping	referring	swum	lighting
		swimming	

The part of the verb that is given first under the head-word, e.g. *galloped, referred, swam,* is the past tense of the verb as in

> The horse galloped along the road.
> He referred to the subject briefly.
> The boy swam the river yesterday.

Where more than one form is allowable both have been given, e.g. *lit, lighted* as in

> She lit (*or* lighted) the candles.

Where three parts of a verb are listed under the headword the second part listed is the past participle, e.g. *swum* as in

> The boy has swum the river three times.

Where only two parts of a verb are listed the past participle is the same as the past tense as in

> The horse has galloped along the road.
> He has already referred to the subject.

The part of the verb given last in every case is the present participle, e.g. *galloping, referring, swimming, lighting* as in

> The horse was galloping along the road.
> He is not referring to her.
> He is swimming well.
> She is lighting the candles.

Many verbs in English can be spelled with either *-ize* or *-ise* as the ending. Which you use is a matter of choice. This guide allows both spellings in the headword — the parts of the verb follow the headword although only the *-z-* form is given.

Words which are very commonly misspelled and so are known pitfalls, e.g. **accommodation, assassinate, occasionally, immediate**, are printed in **bold type**.

Underneath certain words are sentences or phrases in *italic type*. This is to help the user distinguish between words which are liable to be confused, e.g.

illegible
*untidy and illegible
handwriting*

eligible
*an eligible bachelor:
eligible for the job*

canvas
*canvas for painting:
a canvas tent*

canvass
to canvass for votes

check
*a police check on cars:
to check the oil:
to check a sum*

cheque
a bank cheque

it's
= it is
It's fine

its
its leg

To provide further assistance these words are listed in alphabetical order at the end of the book with the words with which they are liable to be confused.

American spelling

There are some common variations between British and American spelling:

British English	American English
-our as in **colour, humour**	**-or** as in **color, humor**
-re as in **centre, theatre, metre**	**-er** as in **center, theater, meter**
-ae as in **haemoglobin, anaemia**	**-e** as in **hemoglobin, anemia**

NB   There is a growing tendency in British English for the **ae** in such words to become **e** as in **medieval, encyclop(a)edia**.

-ogue as in **catalogue**	**-og** as in **catalog**

NB   Many words of this type can be spelled either **-ogue** or **-og** in American English as **prologue/prolog, dialogue/dialog**.

-ll- as in **travelling, equalled**	**-l-** as in **traveling, equaled**
-pp- as in **kidnapped, worshipping**	**-p-** as in **kidnaped, worshiping**
-l- as in **skilful, wilful**	**-ll-** as in **skillful, willful**

Pronunciation guide

a	as in **hat**	ō	as in **toe**
ä	as in **path**	o͝o	as in **book**
à	as in **play**	o͞o	as in **moon**
e	as in **leg**	ow	as in **shout**
ē	as in **clean**	u	as in **run**
i	as in **stick**	ū	as in **tune**
ī	as in **side**	ə	as in **infant**
ö	as in **fall**	sh	as in **ship**

A stress mark ' indicates that the syllable following is pronounced with most emphasis.

Abbreviations

adv	adverb	*compar*	comparative
pl(s)	plural(s)	*superl*	superlative

A

a

a boy: a house:
a usual event

aback

abacus
 pl abacuses

abandon
 abandoned
 abandoning

abase
 abased
 abasing

abasement

abashed

abate
 abated
 abating

abatement

abattoir

abbess
 pl abbesses

abbey
 pl abbeys

abbot

abbreviate
 abbreviated
 abbreviating

abbreviation

abdicate
 abdicated
 abdicating

abdication

abdomen

abdominal

abduct

abduction

abet

abetted
abetting
abeyance
abhor
 abhorred
 abhorring
abhorrence
abhorrent
abide by
 abided by
 abode by
 abiding by
abiding
ability
 pl abilities
abject
ablaze
able
 adv ably
ablutions
abnormal
 adv abnormally
abnormality
 pl abnormalities
aboard
 aboard ship
abode
abolish
abolition
abolitionist
abominable
 adv abominably
abominate
 abominated
 abominating
abomination
aboriginal
aborigine
abort

abortion
abortive
abound
about
above
abrasion
abrasive
 adv abrasively
abreast
abridge
 abridged
 abridging
abridgement,
 abridgment
abroad

He goes abroad on
holiday: There's a
rumour abroad

abrupt
abruptness
abscess
 pl abscesses
abscond
absence
absent
absentee
absent-minded
absolute
 adv absolutely
absoluteness
absolution
absolve
 absolved
 absolving
absorb
absorbent
absorption
abstain
abstainer

1

abstemious
abstention
abstinence
abstract
abstruse
  adv abstrusely
absurd
absurdity
  pl absurdities
abundance
abundant
abuse
  abused
  abusing
abusive
  adv abusively
abysmal
  adv **abysmally**
abyss
  pl abysses
acacia
academic
  adv academically
academy
  pl academies
accede
  acceded
  acceding
accelerate
  accelerated
  accelerating
acceleration
accelerator
accent
accentuate
  accentuated
  accentuating
accept
  to accept a present:

to accept his decision
acceptable
acceptance
access
  access to the
  motorway: He has
  access to his children
accessibility
accessible
  adv accessibly
accession
accessory
  pl **accessories**
accident
accidental
  adv accidentally
acclaim
acclamation
acclimatization,
  -isation
acclimatize, -ise
  acclimatized
  acclimatizing
accommodate
  accommodated
  accommodating
accommodation
accompaniment
accompanist
accompany
  accompanied
  accompanying
accomplice
accomplish
accomplished
accomplishment
accord
accordance
according

accordingly
accordion
accost
account
accountable
accountant
accoutrements
accredited
accrue
  accrued
  accruing
accumulate
  accumulated
  accumulating
accumulation
accumulator
accuracy
accurate
  adv accurately
accursed
accusation
accuse
  accused
  accusing
accuser
accustomed
ace
acetylene
ache
  ached
  aching
achieve
  achieved
  achieving
achievement
acid
acidity
acknowledge
  acknowledged

acknowledging

acknowledgement,
acknowledgment

acme

the acme of perfection

acne

acne on his face

acorn

acoustic

adv acoustically

acoustics

acquaint

acquaintance

acquiesce

acquiesced

acquiescing

acquiescence

acquire

acquired

acquiring

acquisition

acquisitive

acquit

acquitted

acquitting

acquittal

acre

acreage

acrid

acrimonious

acrimony

acrobat

acrobatic

adv acrobatically

acronym

across

acrostic

act

action

actionable

activate

activated

activating

active

adv actively

activity

pl activities

actor

actress

pl actresses

actual

adv actually

actuary

pl actuaries

actuate

actuated

actuating

acumen

acupuncture

acute

adv acutely

acuteness

ad

an ad in the paper

adage

adamant

Adam's apple

adapt

adaptable

adaptation

adapter

the adapter of a play
for TV

adaptor

an adaptor for an
electrical plug

add

to add two numbers

added

adding

addendum

pl addenda

adder

addict

addicted

addiction

addictive

addition

the addition of the
numbers: an addition
to the family

additional

adv additionally

address

pl addresses

addressed

addressing

addressee

adenoids

adept

adequacy

adequate

adv adequately

adhere

adhered

adhering

adherence

adherent

adhesion

adhesive

adjacent

adjectival

adv adjectivally

adjective

adjoin

adjoined

adjoining

3

adjourn
adjournment
adjudicate
  adjudicated
  adjudicating
adjudication
adjudicator
adjunct
adjust
adjustable
adjustment
adjutant
ad-lib
  ad-libbed
  ad-libbing
administer
  administered
  administering
administrate
  administrated
  administrating
administration
administrative
administrator
admirable
  adv admirably
admiral
admiralty
admiration
admire
  admired
  admiring
admirer
admiring
admissible
  adv admissibly
admission
admit
  admitted

admitting
admittance
admonish
admonition
admonitory
ado
adolescence
adolescent
adopt
adoption
adoptive
adorable
  adv adorably
adoration
adore
  adored
  adoring
adorn
adornment
adrift
adroit
adulation
adult
adulterate
  adulterated
  adulterating
adulteration
adulterer
adulteress
  pl adulteresses
adultery
advance
  advanced
  advancing
advancement
advantage
advantageous
advent
adventitious

adventure
adventurer
adventurous
adverb
adverbial
  adv adverbially
adversary
  pl adversaries
adverse
  in adverse
  circumstances
  adv adversely
adversity
  pl adversities
advert
advertise
  advertised
  advertising
advertisement
advice
  She gave him good
  advice: an advice
  from the bank
advisability
advisable
advise
  to advise him to go
  advised
  advising
advisory
advocate
  advocated
  advocating
adze
aeon, eon
aerate
  aerated
  aerating
aerial

4

aerie *see* eyrie
aerobatics
aerodrome
aeroplane
aerosol
aesthetic
*That colour scheme is
not very aesthetic*
adv **aesthetically**
affability
affable
adv **affably**
affair
affect
*Will her nervousness
affect her playing?*
affectation
affection
affectionate
adv **affectionately**
affidavit
affiliate
affiliated
affiliating
affiliation
affinity
pl **affinities**
affirm
affirmation
affirmative
affix
afflict
affliction
affluence
affluent
the affluent society
afford
afforestation
affray

affront
afloat
afoot
aforesaid
afraid
aft
after
aftermath
afternoon
afterthought
afterwards
again
against
agate
age
aged
aging, ageing
agency
pl **agencies**
agenda
pl **agendas**
agent
aggravate
aggravated
aggravating
aggravation
aggregate
aggression
aggressive
adv **aggressively**
aggrieved
aghast
agile
adv **agilely**
agility
agitate
agitated
agitating
agitation

agitator
agnostic
agnosticism
ago
agog
agonized, -ised
agonizing, -ising
agony
agoraphobia
agree
agreed
agreeing
agreeable
adv **agreeably**
agreement
agricultural
adv **agriculturally**
agriculture
aground
ague
ahead
aid
ail
What ails her?
ailed
ailing
aileron
aim
aimless
air
fresh air
aired
airing
airborne
aircraft
airless
airport
airy
adv **airily**

aisle

the aisle in the church

ajar

akimbo

akin

alacrity

alarm

alarming

alarmist

alas!

albatross

pl albatrosses

albino

pl albinos

album

alchemy

alcohol

alcoholic

alcoholism

alcove

alderman

ale

two pints of ale

alert

alfalfa

alfresco

algae

algebra

algebraic

alias

pl aliases

alibi

pl **alibis**

alien

alienate

alienating

alight

alighted, alit

alighting

align

aligned

aligning

alignment

alike

alimentary

alit *see* alight

alive

alkali

alkaline

all

all of you:
all in red

allay

to allay his fears

allayed

allaying

allegation

allege

alleged

alleging

allegiance

allegorical

adv allegorically

allegory

Pilgrim's Progress is
an allegory

pl allegories

allergic

allergy

an allergy to certain
foods

pl allergies

alleviate

alleviated

alleviating

alleviation

alley

a bowling alley: He
ran down the alley

pl alleys

alliance

alligator

alliterate

Sand, sea and sun
alliterate

alliterated

alliterating

alliteration

allocate

allocated

allocating

allocation

allot

allotted

allotting

allotment

allow

allowed

allowing

allowable

allowance

alloy

all right

allude

He did not allude
to the matter

alluded

alluding

allure

allured

alluring

allusion

He made no allusion
to the matter

alluvial

ally
  pl allies
allied
allying
almanac
almighty
almond
almost
alms
aloft
alone
along
aloof
aloofness
aloud
alpha
alphabet
alphabetical
  adv alphabetically
alpine
already
alsatian
also
altar
  *the bridegroom at
  the altar*
alter
  *to alter your plans:
  to alter a dress*
altered
altering
alteration
  *alteration to my
  plans: alteration to
  my dress*
altercation
  *The altercation ended
  in blows*
al'ternate

adv alternately
  *alternately hot
  and cold*
'alternate
alternated
alternating
alternative
  adv alternatively
  *You could go by bus —
  alternatively you
  could go by train*
although
altimeter
altitude
alto
altogether
altruism
altruistic
  adv altruistically
aluminium
always
am *see* be
amalgam
amalgamate
  amalgamated
  amalgamating
amalgamation
amass
amateur
  an amateur golf player
amateurish
  *an amateurish attempt
  at building a shed*
amaze
  amazed
  amazing
amazement
ambassador
ambassadress

  pl ambassa-
    dresses
amber
ambidexterous,
  ambidextrous
ambiguity
  pl ambiguities
ambiguous
ambition
ambitious
amble
  ambled
  ambling
ambrosia
ambulance
ambush
  pl ambushes
amenable
amend
  to amend the law
amendments
amenity
  pl amenities
amethyst
amiable
  an amiable young man
  adv amiably
amicable
  *on amicable terms:
  an amicable separation*
  adv amicably
amid, amidst
amiss
amity
ammonia
ammunition
amnesia
amnesty
  pl amnesties

amoeba
amok, amuck
run amok
among, amongst
Divide the chocolate among all four
amoral
She is quite amoral — she doesn't know right from wrong
amorous
amorousness
amount
amp, ampère
amphibian
amphibious
amphitheatre
ample
adv amply
amplification
amplifier
amplify
amplified
amplifying
amplitude
amputate
amputated
amputating
amputation
amuck *see* amok
amulet
amuse
amused
amusing
amusement
an
an art: an orange: an honour
anachronism

anachronistic
anaemia
anaemic
anaesthetic
anaesthetist
anagram
analogous
analogy
pl analogies
analyse
analysed
analysing
analysis
anarchist
anarchy
anathema
anatomical
adv anatomically
anatomist
anatomy
ancestor
ancestral
ancestress
pl ancestresses
ancestry
anchor
anchored
anchoring
anchorage
anchovy
pl anchovies
ancient
ancillary
anecdotal
anecdote
anemometer
anemone
aneroid
barometer

angel
an angel from heaven: Be an angel and help me with this
angelic
adv angelically
angelica
anger
angered
angering
angina
angle
an angle of 90°: a new angle on the story: to angle for a job: to angle the camera
angled
angling
angler
Anglican
anglicize, -ise
anglicized
anglicizing
Anglo-Saxon
angora
angry
adv **angrily**
anguish
anguished
angular
animal
animate
animated
animating
animation
animosity
aniseed
ankle
annals

The Annals of the Parish: in the annals of crime

an'nex
to annex a country

'annex, annexe
build an annexe to the house

annihilate
annihilated
annihilating
annihilation
anniversary
pl anniversaries
annotate
annotated
annotating
annotation
announce
announced
announcing
announcement
announcer
annoy
annoyed
annoying
annoyance
annual
pl annuals
Christmas annuals
adv **annually**
annuity
pl annuities
annul
annulled
annulling
annulment
anoint
anomalous

anomaly
pl anomalies
anon
anonymity
anonymous
anorak
another
answer
answered
answering
answerable
ant
He was bitten by an ant
antagonism
antagonist
antagonistic
adv antagonistically
antagonize, -ise
antagonized
antagonizing
Antarctic
antecedent
antediluvian
antelope
antenatal
antenna
pl antennae, antennas
anteroom
anthem
anthology
pl anthologies
anthracite
anthrax
anthropoid
anthropological
anthropologist

anthropology
antibiotic
anticipate
anticipated
anticipating
anticipation
anticlimax
anticlockwise
antics
anticyclone
antidote
antihistamine
antipathy
antipodes
antiquated
antiquated ideas
antique
an antique table: a valuable antique
antiseptic
antisocial
antithesis
pl antitheses
antler
anvil
anxiety
pl anxieties
anxious
any
anybody
anyhow
anyone
anything
anywhere
apart
apartheid
apartment
apathetic
adv apathetically

apathy
ape
  aped
  aping
aperture
apex
  pl apexes, apices
aphid
apiary
  pl apiaries
apices *see* apex
apiece
aplomb
apocryphal
apologetic
  adv apologetically
apologize, -ise
  apologized
  apologizing
apology
  pl apologies
apoplectic
apoplexy
apostle
apostrophe
apothecary
  pl apothecaries
appal
  appalled
  appalling
apparatus
apparel
apparent
  adv **apparently**
apparition
appeal
  appealed
  appealing
appear

appeared
appearing
appearance
appease
  appeased
  appeasing
appendicitis
appendix
  pl appendixes,
    appendices
appertain
  appertained
  appertaining
appetite
appetizing, -ising
applaud
applause
apple
appliance
applicable
applicant
application
apply
  applied
  applying
appoint
appointment
apportion
  apportioned
  apportioning
apposite
appraisal
appraise
  appraised
  appraising
appreciable
  adv appreciably
appreciate
  appreciated

appreciating
appreciation
apprehend
apprehension
apprehensive
  adv
  apprehensively
apprentice
apprenticeship
approach
  pl approaches
approachable
approbation
appropriate
  adv appropriately
appropriated
appropriating
approval
approve
  approved
  approving
approximate
  adv
  approximately
approximation
apricot
April
apron
apropos of
apse
apt
  adv aptly
aptitude
aquamarine
aquarium
  pl aquaria
aquatic
aqueduct
aquiline

arable
arbiter
arbitrary
  adv arbitrarily
arbitrate
  arbitrated
  arbitrating
arbitration
arbitrator
arbour
arc
  the arc of a circle:
  arc lamp
arcade
arch
  pl arches
archaeological
archaeologist
archaeology
archaic
archangel
archbishop
archer
archery
archipelago
  pl archipelagos,
    archipelagoes
architect
architectural
  adv
    architecturally
architecture
archives
Arctic
ardent
ardour
arduous
arduousness
are *see* be

area
  pl areas
arena
aren't
  = are not
argosy
  pl argosies
arguable
  adv **arguably**
argue
  argued
  arguing
argument
argumentative
  adv argumenta-
    tively
aria
  pl arias
arid
arise
  arose
  A problem arose
  arisen
  A problem has arisen
  arising
aristocracy
aristocrat
aristocratic
  adv
    aristocratically
arithmetic
arithmetical
  adv arithmetically
ark
  Noah's ark
arm
armada
  pl armadas
armadillo

  pl armadillos
armaments
armchair
armistice
armorial
armour
armoured
armoury
army
  pl armies
aroma
  pl aromas
aromatic
arose *see* arise
around
arouse
  aroused
  arousing
arrange
  arranged
  arranging
arrangement
arras
array
  arrayed
  arraying
arrears
arrest
arrival
arrive
  arrived
  arriving
arrogance
arrogant
arrow
arsenal
arsenic
arson
art

artful
adv artfully
artless
artefact,
  artifact
arterial
artery
  pl arteries
artesian well
artichoke
article
articulate
  articulated
  articulating
articulation
artifact *see*
  artefact
artificial
  adv artificially
artificiality
artillery
artisan
artist
  a portrait artist:
  a concert artist
artiste
  a circus artiste
artistic
  adv artistically
artistry
as
asbestos
ascend
  ascended
  ascending
  ascendancy,
  ascendency
  ascendant,
  ascendent

ascent
  the ascent of the
  mountain: ascent
  to the throne
ascertain
ascetic
  Monks lead
  ascetic lives
  adv ascetically
ascribe
  ascribed
  ascribing
ash
ashamed
ashen
ashes
ashore
aside
asinine
ask
askance
askew
asleep
asp
asparagus
aspect
asperity
asphalt
asphyxia
asphyxiate
  asphyxiated
  asphyxiating
asphyxiation
aspidistra
aspiration
aspire
  aspired
  aspiring
aspirin

ass
  pl asses
assail
  assailed
  assailing
assailant
assassin
assassinate
  assassinated
  assassinating
assassination
assault
assay
  an assay of gold
assemble
  assembled
  assembling
assembly
  pl assemblies
assent
  The Queen gave her
  assent to the new Bill
assert
assertion
assertive
  adv assertively
assess
assessment
assessor
asset
  pl assets
assiduous
assign
  assigned
  assigning
assignation
assignment
assimilate
  assimilated

assimilating
assimilation
assist
assistance
assistant
assizes
associate
associated
associating
association
assorted
assortment
assuage
assuaged
assuaging
assume
assumed
assuming
assumption
assurance
assure
assured
assuring
asterisk
asthma
asthmatic
adv asthmatically
astonish
astonishment
astound
astrakhan
astral
astray
astride
astringent
astrologer
astrological
adv astrologically
astrology

Astrology deals with the signs of the zodiac

astronaut
astronomer
astronomical
adv astronomically
astronomy
He is studying physics and astronomy

astute
asunder
asylum
at
ate *see* eat
atheism
atheist
athlete
athletic
adv athletically
athletics
atlas
pl atlases
atmosphere
atmospheric
adv atmospherically
atmospherics
atoll
atom
atomic
atone
atoned
atoning
atonement
atrocious
atrocity
pl atrocities

attach
attached
attaching
attaché-case
attachment
attack
attacker
attain
attainable
attainment
attempt
attend
attendance
attendant
attention
attentive
adv attentively
attic
attire
attired
attiring
attitude
attorney
pl attorneys
attract
attraction
attractive
adv attractively
attributable
attribute
attributed
attributing
aubergine
auburn
auction
auctioneer
audacious
audacity
audibility

audible
  adv audibly
audience
audio-typist
audio-visual
audit
  audited
  auditing
audition
auditor
auditorium
  pl auditoriums,
    auditoria
auditory
augment
augmentation
augur
  augured
  auguring
'August
au'gust
auk
aunt
  her aunt and uncle
aural
  = of hearing
  Her aural faculties
  were impaired
auspices
auspicious
austere
  adv austerely
austerity
authentic
authenticate
  authenticated
  authenticating
authenticity
author

authoritarian
authoritative
authority
  pl authorities
authorization,
  -isation
authorize, -ise
  authorized
  authorizing
autobiographical
autobiography
  pl autobiogra-
    phies
autocrat
autograph
automatic
  adv automatically
automation
automaton
  pl automatons,
    automata
autonomous
autonomy
autopsy
  pl autopsies
autumn
autumnal
auxiliary
  pl auxiliaries
avail
  availed
  availing
availability
available
avalanche
avarice
avaricious
avenge
  avenged

avenging
avenger
avenue
average
  averaged
  averaging
averse
  I'm not averse to work
aversion
avert
aviary
  pl aviaries
aviation
aviator
avid
avidity
avoid
avoidable
  adv avoidably
avoidance
avoirdupois
avow
avowal
await
awake
awaken
  awakened
  awakening
award
aware
awareness
away
awe
awesome
awful
  adv awfully
awfulness
awkward
  adv awkwardly

awkwardness
awl
the cobbler's awl
awning
awoke
awry
axe
pl axes
axes for chopping wood
axed
axing
axis
turning on an axis
axle
azure

B

babble
babbled
babbling
baboon
baby
pl babies
babyhood
babysit
babysat
babysitting
babysitter
bachelor
bachelorhood
bacillus
pl bacilli
back
backer
backgammon
background
backing

backward
backwards
bacon
bacteria
bacterial
bacteriologist
bacteriology
bad
a bad boy
compar worse
superl worst
bade *see* bid
badger
badgered
badgering
badminton
baffle
baffled
baffling
bag
bagged
bagging
bagatelle
baggage
baggy
bagpipes
bail
to pay bail: to bail him out of prison
bailed
bailing
bailiff
bait
baited
He baited his line
baiting
baize
bake
baked

baking
baker
bakery
pl bakeries
balance
balanced
balancing
balcony
pl balconies
bald
balderdash
bale
a bale of cotton
baleful
adv balefully
bale out
to bale out of an aircraft: to bale out water
baled out
baling out
balk, baulk
balked, baulked
balking, baulking
ball
a ball of wool: a tennis ball: a formal ball
ballad
ballast
ballerina
ballet
ballet shoes
ballistic
balloon
ballot
to vote in a secret ballot
balm

15

balmy
balsa (wood)
balustrade
bamboo
bamboozle
  bamboozled
  bamboozling
ban
  pl bans
  government bans
  on smoking
  banned
  banning
banal
banality
  pl banalities
banana
band
bandage
  bandaged
  bandaging
bandeau
  pl bandeaux
bandit
bandy
  bandied
  bandying
bandy(-legged)
bane
bang
bangle
banish
banishment
banister
banjo
  pl banjos,
    banjoes
bank
banker

bankrupt
bankruptcy
banner
banns
  marriage banns
banquet
bantam
banter
bantering
baptism
baptismal
baptize, -ise
  baptized
  baptizing
bar
  barred
  barring
barb
barbarian
barbaric
  adv barbarically
barbarity
  pl barbarities
barbecue
  barbecued
  barbecuing
barbed
barber
bard
bare
  to bare his teeth
  bared
  baring
bare
  bare legs
barely
bareness
bargain
  bargained

bargaining
barge
  barged
  barging
baritone
bark
barley
barn
  hay in the barn
barnacle
barometer
baron
  He has the title
  of baron: Baron Smith
  of Baberton
baroness
  pl baronesses
baronet
baronetcy
barracks
barrage
barrel
barren
  barren fields:
  a barren woman
barrenness
barricade
  barricaded
  barricading
barrier
barring
barrister
barrow
barter
  bartered
  bartering
basalt
base
  This paint has an oil

base: the base of his spine: to use the office as a base: to base an argument on facts

based

basing

baseball

basement

bashful

adv bashfully

basic

adv **basically**

basil

basilisk

basin

basis

pl bases

bask

basket

basket-ball

bass [bās]

the bass singer

pl basses

the basses in the choir

bass [bas]

pl bass

The fisherman caught several bass

bassoon

baste

basted

basting

bastion

bat

batted

batting

batch

pl batches

bated

with bated breath

bath

to bath the baby

bathed

bathing

bathe

to bathe in the sea: to bathe a wound

bathed

bathing

batik

batman

baton

a policeman's baton

batsman

battalion

batten

The joiner put up a batten

batter

battered

battering

battery

pl batteries

battle

battled

battling

battle-axe

battlement

bauble

baulk *see* balk

bawl

The child began to bawl

bay

bayed

baying

bayonet

bazaar, bazar

an Eastern bazaar: a church bazaar

be

to be helpful

am, is, are

was, were

been

he has been: they have been

being

He is being funny: a human being

beach

a sandy beach

pl beaches

beacon

bead

beadle

beagle

beak

beaker

beam

bean

a French bean

bear

a brown bear: I can't bear the noise: to bear the strain: to bear children

bore

He bore it

borne

I have borne it

bearing

bearable

beard

bearded

17

bearer
bearing
beast
beastliness
beastly
beat
  *to beat someone
  at tennis*
  beat
  He beat her
  beaten
  He has beaten her
beatific
  adv beatifically
beau [bō]
  *Her latest beau
  is very handsome*
beautiful
  adv beautifully
beautify
  beautified
  beautifying
beauty
  pl beauties
beaver
beaver away
  beavered away
  beavering away
becalmed
became *see*
  become
because
beck
beckon
  beckoned
  beckoning
become
  became
  He became a doctor

become
  *He has become a
  doctor*
  becoming
becoming
bed
  bedded
  bedding
bedlam
bedraggled
bedridden
bee
  a honey bee
beech
  a beech tree
  pl beeches
beef
beefeater
beefy
been *see* be
beer
  a pint of beer
beet
  sugar beet
beetle
  beetling
beetroot
befall
  befell
  What befell him?
befallen
  What has befallen you?
  befalling
befit
  befitted
  befitting
before
beforehand
befriend

beg
  begged
  begging
began *see* begin
beget
  begot
  begotten
beggar
  beggared
  beggaring
beggarly
begin
  began
  It began to rain
  begun
  It has begun to rain
  beginning
begrudge
  begrudged
  begrudging
beguile
  beguiled
  beguiling
begun *see* begin
behalf
behave
  behaved
  behaving
behaviour
behead
behest
behind
behold
  beheld
  beholding
  beholden
being *see* be
belabour
  belaboured

belabouring
belated
belch
beleaguer
  beleaguered
  beleaguering
belfry
  pl belfries
belie
  belied
  belying
belief
  to show his belief in God
believe
  to believe in God
  believed
  believing
belittle
  belittled
  belittling
bell
  a church bell
belle
  the belle of the ball
bellicose
belligerent
bellow
  Bulls bellow
bellows
belly
  pl bellies
belong
  belonged
  belonging
belongings
beloved
below
  below the level

belt
belying *see* belie
bemoan
  bemoaned
  bemoaning
bench
  pl benches
bend
  bent
  bending
beneath
benediction
benefactor
  adv **beneficially**
beneficiary
  pl beneficiaries
benefit
  benefited
  benefiting
benevolence
benevolent
benign
bent *see* bend
bequeath
  bequeathed
  bequeathing
bequest
berate
  berated
  berating
bereaved
bereavement
bereft
beret
  She wore a blue beret
berry
  a holly berry
  pl berries
berserk

berth
  a berth on a ship
berthed
berthing
beryl
beseech
beset
  beset
  besetting
beside
  beside the tree
besides
  Others, besides him, will come
besiege
  besieged
  besieging
besotted with
bespoke
best *see* good
bestial
  adv **bestially**
bestir
  bestirred
  bestirring
bestow
bet
  bet, (*rare*) betted
  betting
betray
  betrayed
  betraying
betrayal
betroth
betrothal
betrothed
better
  bettered
  bettering

better *see* good
betting *see* bet
between

Divide the chocolate between you and your sister: between London and New York

bevel
bevelled
bevelling
beverage
bevy
pl bevies
bewail
bewailed
bewailing
beware
bewilder
bewildered
bewildering
bewitch
beyond
bias
biased, biassed
biasing, biassing
bib
bible
biblical
bibliographer
bibliography
pl bibliographies
bibliophile
bicentenary
biceps
bicker
bickered
bickering
bicycle
bid

bid, bade [bad]

He bid £3: He bade him farewell

bidding
biennial
adv biennially
bier
a funeral bier
big
compar bigger
superl biggest
bigamist
bigamous
bigamy
bigger, biggest
see big
bight
= a bay
the Great Australian Bight
bigot
bigoted
bigotry
bike
bikini
pl bikinis
bilateral
bilberry
pl bilberries
bile
bilious
biliousness
bilge
bilingual
bill
billet
billeted
billeting
billet doux

billiards
billow
bin
binary
bind
bound
books bound in leather: to be bound to lose
binding
bingo
binoculars
biographer
biographical
biography
pl biographies
biological
adv biologically
biologist
biology
birch
pl birches
bird
Biro ®
birth
the birth of her child
birthday
biscuit
bisect
bishop
bishopric
bison
bit *see* bite
bitch
pl bitches
bite
Did the dog bite the man?
bit

The dog bit me
bitten
The dog has bitten me
bitter
bivouac
bivouacked
bivouacking
bi-weekly
bizarre

clowns wearing bizarre costumes: We met in bizarre circumstances

blab
blabbed
blabbing
black
blackboard
blacken
blackened
blackening
blackguard
blackmail
blackmailed
blackmailing
blackmailer
bladder
blade
blame
blamed
blaming
blameless
blancmange
bland
blandishments
blank
blanket
blanketed
blanketing
blare

blared
blaring
blarney
blaspheme
blasphemed
blaspheming
blasphemous
blasphemy
blast
blast-off
blatant
blaze
blazed
blazing
blazer
blazon
blazoned
blazoning
bleach
pl **bleaches**
bleak
bleakness
bleary
bleat
bleed
bled
bleeding
bleep
blemish
pl **blemishes**
blend
blender
bless
blessed
blessing
blew *see* blow
blight
blind
blindfold

blindness
blink
blinkers
bliss
blissful
adv **blissfully**
blister
blistered
blistering
blithe
adv **blithely**
blitz
blizzard
bloated
bloater
blob
bloc
the Eastern bloc of nations
block
a block of wood: a block of flats: to block a pipe
blockade
blockaded
blockading
blond
blond hair
blonde
She's a beautiful blonde
blood
bloodhound
bloodshed
bloody
bloom
bloomed
blooming
blossom

blossomed
blossoming
blot
blotted
blotting
blotch
pl blotches
blotchy
blotter
blouse
blow
blew
He blew the trumpet
blown
He has blown the trumpet
blowing
blowy
blowzy
blubber
bludgeon
bludgeoned
bludgeoning
blue
a blue sky
blueprint
bluff
blunder
blundered
blundering
blunderbuss
pl blunderbusses
blunt
blur
blurred
blurring
blurt out
blush
pl blushes

bluster
blustered
blustering
boa
boa constrictor
boar
a wild boar
board
a board of directors: a wooden board: to board a ship: to board up a window: to board at a guest house
boarder
boast
to boast about his achievements
boastful
adv boastfully
boat
boater
boating
boatswain, bosun
bob
bobbed
bobbing
bobbin
bobsleigh
bode
boded
boding
bodice
bodily
bodkin
body
pl bodies
bodyguard
boffin
bog down

bogged down
bogging down
bogey
pl bogeys
boggle
boggled
boggling
bogus
boil
boiled
boiling
boiler
boisterous
bold
bollard
bolster up
bolstered up
bolstering up
bolt
bomb
bombed
bombing
bombard
bombardment
bombastic
bomber
bombshell
bond
bondage
bone
bonfire
bonnet
bonny
a plump, bonny baby
bonus
pl bonuses
bony
bony elbows: bony fist

22

boo
  booed
  booing
booby
book
bookie
  to bet with a bookie
book-keeping
booklet
boom
  boomed
  booming
boomerang
boon
boor
  an ill-mannered boor
boorish
boost
  to boost his self-
  confidence: to boost
  his resistance
  to polio
booster
boot
bootee
  a baby's bootee
booth
  pl booths
booty
  booty from the
  wrecked ship
border
  bordered
  bordering
bore see bear
bore
  He's a tiresome bore:
  to bore a hole: to
  bore him with a long
  speech

bored
  a bored listener
boring
boredom
born
  His mother died
  when he was born
borne see bear
borough
  Boroughs have
  royal charters
borrow
borzoi
bosom
boss
  pl bosses
bosun see
  boatswain
botanical
  adv botanically
botanist
botany
botch
both
bother
  bothered
  bothering
bothy
  pl bothies
bottle
  bottled
  bottling
bottleneck
bottom
boudoir
bough
  the bough of a tree
bought see buy
boulder

bounce
  bounced
  bouncing
bouncer
bound see bind
bound
  bounded
  The dog bounded
  over to us
  bounding
boundary
  pl boundaries
boundless
bounteous
bountiful
bounty
  pl bounties
bouquet
  a bouquet of flowers
bourgeois
bout
boutique
bovine
bow [bow]
  to bow one's head
  bowed
  bowing
bow [bō]
  a bow in her hair
bowels
bower
bowl
bowler
bowls
box
  pl boxes
boxer
boy
  a fair-haired boy

23

boycott
  boycotted
  boycotting
boyhood
boyish
boyishness
bra
brace
  braced
  bracing
bracelet
braces
bracing
bracken
bracket
  bracketed
  bracketing
brackish
bradawl
brae (*Scots*)
  a steep brae
brag
  bragged
  bragging
braid
braille
brain
  brained
  braining
brainwave
brainy
braise
  braised
  braising
brake
  to put on the car brake: to brake going round a corner
  braked

braking
bramble
bran
branch
  pl branches
brand
brandish
brand-new
brandy
  pl brandies
brass
  pl brasses
brassière
  What size of brassière?
brassy
brat
bravado
brave
  adv bravely
  braved
  braving
bravery
bravo
brawl
brawn
brawny
bray
  The ass began to bray
  brayed
  braying
brazen
brazen it out
  brazened it out
  brazening it out
brazier
  a brazier of burning coal
brazil-nut

breach
  a breach of the peace: a breach in the defences: to breach their defence
  pl breaches
bread
  a loaf of bread
breadth
breadwinner
break
  to break a leg
  broke
    He broke a cup
  broken
    He has broken a cup
  breaking
breakable
breakage
breaker
breakfast
break-in
bream
breast
breath
  a breath of air: take a breath
breathalyser
breathe
  to breathe in
  breathed
  breathing
breathless
bred *see* breed
breech
  the breech of a gun: a breech delivery of a child
breeches

breed
bred
He bred cocker spaniels
breeding
breeze
breezy
brethren
brevity
brew
brewery
pl breweries
briar, brier
bribe
bribed
bribing
bribery
bric-à-brac
brick
bridal
bridal party
bride
bridegroom
bridesmaid
bridge
bridged
bridging
bridle
*a horse's bridle:
to bridle in anger*
bridled
bridling
brief
briefs
brier *see* briar
brigade
brigand
bright
brighten

brightened
brightening
brilliance
brilliant
brim
brimmed
brimming
brimful
brimstone
brine
bring
brought
bringing
brink
briny
brisk
bristle
bristled
bristling
bristly
brittle
broach
to broach the subject
broached
broaching
broad
broadcast
broadcast
broadcasting
broaden
broadened
broadening
brocade
broccoli
brochure
brogue
broil
broke, broken *see* break

broker
bronchitic
bronchitis
brontosaurus
bronze
bronzed
brooch
a silver brooch
pl brooches
brood
brook
broom
broth
brother
brotherhood
brother-in-law
pl brothers-in-law
brotherly
brought *see* bring
brow
browbeat
browbeat
browbeating
brown
brownie
pl brownies
browse
browsed
browsing
bruise
bruised
bruising
brunette
brunt
brush
pl brushes
brusque
adv brusquely

brusqueness
Brussels sprouts
brutal
  adv brutally
brutality
brute
brutish
bubble
  bubbled
  bubbling
bubbly
buccaneer
buccaneering
buck
bucket
buckle
  buckled
  buckling
buckler
buckshot
bud
  budded
  budding
Buddhism
Buddhist
budge
  budged
  budging
budgerigar
budget
  budgeted
  budgeting
budgie
buff
buffalo
  pl buffaloes
buffer
buffet ['bŏŏfã]
  the station buffet:

a buffet supper
buffet ['bufit]
Heavy waves
buffet the boat
buffeted
buffeting
buffoon
buffoonery
bug
  bugged
  bugging
bugbear
bugle
bugler
build
  built
  building
  builder
built-up
bulb
bulbous
bulge
  bulged
  bulging
bulk
bulky
bulldog
bulldoze
  bulldozed
  bulldozing
  bulldozer
bullet
bulletin
bullion
bullock
bull's-eye
bully
  pl bullies
bullied

bullying
bulrush
  pl bulrushes
bulwark
bumble-bee
bump
bumper
bumpkin
bumptious
bumptiousness
bunch
  pl bunches
bundle
  bundled
  bundling
bung
bungalow
  pl bungalows
bungle
  bungled
  bungling
bunion
bunk
bunk-bed
bunker
bunkum
bunny
  pl bunnies
bunting
buoy
  a mooring buoy
buoyancy
buoyant
bur *see* burr
burden
  burdened
  burdening
bureau
  pl bureaux,

bureaus
bureaucracy
  pl bureaucracies
bureaucratic
burgh
  *Burgh is a Scots
  form of borough*
burglar
burglary
  pl burglaries
burgle
  burgled
  burgling
burial
buried *see* bury
burlesque
burly
burn
  burnt, burned
  burning
burner
burnish
burr, bur
burrow
burst
  burst
  bursting
bury
  to bury the corpse
  buried
  burying
bus
  pl buses
bush
  pl bushes
bushy
busier, busiest
  see busy
business

pl businesses
busk
busker
bust
bustle
  bustled
  bustling
busy
  compar busier
  superl busiest
  adv busily
but
  *no-one but her:
  But I didn't know*
butcher
butler
butt
  to butt in
butter
buttercup
butterfly
  pl butterflies
butterscotch
buttocks
button
buttoned
  buttoning
buttonhole
buttress
  pl buttresses
buxom
buy
  to buy a new car
  bought
  buying
buyer
buzz
buzzard
buzzer

by
  *written by him:
  Stand by me!*
bye
  a bye in cricket
bye-law, by-law
by-election
bygone
bypass
  bypassed
  bypassing
bystander

C

cab
cabaret
cabbage
cabin
cabinet
cable
  cabled
  cabling
cache
  a cache of jewels
cackle
  cackled
  cackling
cacophonous
cacophony
cactus
  pl cacti, cactuses
cad
cadaverous
caddie
  a golf caddie
  pl caddies
caddy
  a tea caddy

pl caddies
cadence
cadet
cadge
  cadged
  cadging
cadger
café
cafeteria
  pl cafeterias
caffeine
caftan *see* kaftan
cage
  caged
  caging
cagey, cagy
cairn
cairngorm
cajole
  cajoled
  cajoling
cajolery
cake
  caked
  caking
calamine
calamitous
calamity
  pl calamities
calcium
calculate
  calculated
  calculating
calculation
calculator
calculus
calendar
calf
  a cow and her calf:

the calf of his leg
  pl calves
calibrate
  calibrated
  calibrating
calibre
calico
call
calligraphy
callipers,
  calipers
callosity
callous
  hard-hearted and
  callous
callow
callus
  a callus on the skin
  pl calluses
calm
calmness
calorie
calorimeter
calumny
  pl calumnies
calve
  When will the
  cow calve?
  calved
  calving
calypso
  pl calypsos
camber
came *see* come
camel
cameo
  pl cameos
camera
  pl cameras

camomile
camouflage
  camouflaged
  camouflaging
camp
campaign
  campaigned
  campaigning
campanology
camping
campsite
campus
  pl campuses
can
  could
  He could go now
can
  canned
  They canned
  the tomatoes
  canning
canal
canary
  pl canaries
canasta
cancan
cancel
  cancelled
  cancelling
cancer
cancerous
candid
candidacy
candidate
candied
candle
candlestick
candlewick
candour

candy
  pl candies
cane
  caned
  caning
canine
caning
canister
canker
cannabis
canned *see* can
cannery
  pl canneries
cannibal
cannibalism
cannon
  a cannon in battle
cannonball
cannon into
  cannoned into
  cannoning into
cannot
canoe
  pl canoes
canon
  a deacon and a canon:
  a canon of the
  saints: a law or canon

cañon *see* canyon
canonization,
  -isation
canonize, -ise
  canonized
  canonizing
canopy
  pl canopies
cant
  jargon and cant:
  a cant or slope:

Did the boat cant?
canted
canting
can't
  = cannot
  I can't go
cantankerous
cantata
  pl cantatas
canteen
canter
  cantered
  cantering
cantilever bridge
canton
canvas
  canvas for painting:
  a canvas tent
  pl canvases
canvass
  to canvass for votes
  canvassed
  canvassing
canyon, cañon
cap
  capped
  capping
capability
  pl capabilities
capable
capacious
capacitor
capacity
  pl capacities
cape
caper
  capered
  capering
capercaillie,

capercailzie
capillary
  pl capillaries
capital
capitalism
capitalist
capitalistic
capitalize, -ise
  capitalized
  capitalizing
capitulate
  capitulated
  capitulating
capitulation
capon
capped *see* cap
caprice
capricious
capsize
  capsized
  capsizing
capstan
capsule
captain
  captained
  captaining
captaincy
  pl captaincies
caption
captious
captivate
  captivated
  captivating
captive
captivity
captor
capture
  captured
  capturing

29

car
carafe
caramel
carat
18 carat gold
caravan
caravanserai
caraway
carbohydrate
carbolic
carbon
carbuncle
**carburettor,
  carburetter**
carcase,
  carcass
card
cardboard
cardiac
cardigan
cardinal
care
  cared
  caring
carefree
careful
  adv carefully
carefulness
careless
carelessness
career
  careered
  careering
caress
  pl caresses
  caressed
  caressing
caretaker
careworn

cargo
  pl cargoes
caribou
caricature
caricaturist
caries
carillon
carmine
carnage
carnation
carnival
carnivore
carnivorous
carol
  carolled
  carolling
carouse
  caroused
  carousing
carp
carpenter
carpentry
carpet
  carpeted
  carpeting
carriage
carried *see* carry
carrier
carrion
carrot
  grated carrot
carry
  carried
  carrying
cart
  a horse and cart
cartilage
  cartilage in the knee
cartography

carton
  a carton of milk
cartoon
  a Walt Disney cartoon
cartoonist
cartridge
  *a cartridge for a
  gun: film cartridge*
cartwheel
carve
  carved
  carving
cascade
  cascaded
  cascading
case
  cased
  casing
casement
cash
  *to cash a cheque:
  ready cash*
cashew
cashier
  cashiered
  cashiering
cashmere
casino
  pl casinos
cask
casket
casserole
cassette
cassock
cast
  *the cast of a play:
  a cast in his eye:
  to cast a play:
  to cast a glance*

cast
casting
castanets
castaway
caste
a social caste
caster *see* castor
castigate
castigated
castigating
castle
cast-off
castor, caster
castor-oil
castor, caster
sugar
castrate
castrated
castrating
casual
adv casually
casualty
pl casualties
cat
cataclysm
catacomb
catalogue
catalogued
cataloguing
catalyst
catamaran
catapult
cataract
catarrh
catastrophe
catastrophic
adv
catastrophically
catch

caught
catching
catchment
catchy
catechism
categorical
adv categorically
category
pl categories
cater
catered
catering
caterer
caterpillar
caterwauling
cathedral
catherine-wheel
cathode ray tube
catholic
Catholic
catkin
cattle
caught *see* catch
cauldron
cauliflower
cause
caused
causing
causeway
caustic
adv caustically
cauterize, -ise
cauterized
cauterizing
caution
cautionary
cautious
cavalcade
cavalier

*Cavaliers and
Roundheads: a cavalier
attitude*

cavalry
infantry and cavalry

cave
cave in
caved in
caving in
cavern
cavernous
caviare, caviar
cavil
cavilled
cavilling
cavity
pl cavities
cavort
caw
cayenne
cease
ceased
ceasing
ceaseless
cedar
cede
ceded
ceding
ceiling
*He painted the
ceiling white*

celandine
celebrate
celebrated
celebrating
celebration
celebrity
pl celebrities
celery

celestial
celibacy
celibate
cell

a prison cell: a battery cell: a living cell: a monk's cell

cellist
cello
cellophane
cellular

cellular blankets

celluloid
cellulose

cellulose paint

cement
cemetery

pl **cemeteries**

cenotaph
censor

a film censor: to censor letters

censored
censoring
censorious
censure

to censure a naughty child

censured
censuring
census

pl **censuses**

cent

a dollar and a cent

centaur
centenarian

She is a centenarian

centenary

She celebrated

her centenary

pl **centenaries**

centennial
centigrade
centigramme
centilitre
centimetre
centipede
central

adv **centrally**

centralization, -isation
centralize, -ise
centralized
centralizing
centre
centrifugal
century

pl **centuries**

ceramic
cereal

breakfast cereal: barley and other cereals

cerebral
ceremonial
ceremonious
ceremony

pl **ceremonies**

cerise
certain
certainly
certainty

pl **certainties**

certificate
certify
certified
certifying
cessation

cesspool
chafe

My shoes chafe my heels: to chafe at the delay

chafed
chafing
chaff

to chaff each other good-naturedly

chaffed
chaffing
chaffinch

pl **chaffinches**

chagrin
chain
chained
chaining
chair
chaired
chairing
chairman
chalet
chalice
chalk
chalky
challenge
challenged
challenging
chamber
chamberlain
chameleon
chamois, shammy
champ
champagne
champion
championed
championing
championship

chance
  chanced
  chancing
chancel
chancellor
chancery
chancy
chandelier
change
  changed
  changing
changeable
changeling
channel
  channelled
  channelling
chant
chanty *see* shanty
chaos
chaotic
  adv chaotically
chap
chapel
chaperone
  chaperoned
  chaperoning
chaplain
chapped
chapter
char
  charred
  charring
charabanc
character
characteristic
  adv characteristi-
    cally
characterization,
  -isation

characterize, -ise
  characterized
  characterizing
charade
charcoal
charge
  charged
  charging
  charger
chariot
charioteer
charitable
  adv charitably
charity
  pl charities
charlatan
charm
  charming
charnel-house
chart
  charted
    *They have charted
    the coastline*
  charting
charter
  chartered
    We chartered a plane
  chartering
charwoman
chary
chase
  chased
    The dog chased the cat
  chasing
chasm
chassis
chaste
  a chaste woman
chasten

chastened
  chastening
chastise
  chastised
  chastising
chastisement
chastity
chat
  chatted
  chatting
château
  pl châteaux
chattels
chatter
  chattered
  chattering
chatterbox
chatty
  adv chattily
chauffeur
cheap
  at a cheap price
cheapen
  cheapened
  cheapening
cheat
check
  *a police check on
  cars: to check the
  oil: to check a sum*
checked
  a checked dress
checkmate
check-out
cheek
cheeky
  adv cheekily
cheep
  the cheep of a bird:

to cheep merrily
cheeped
cheeping
cheer
cheered
cheering
cheerful
  adv cheerfully
cheerio
cheerless
cheery
  adv cheerily
cheese
cheeseparing
cheetah
chef
chemical
  adv chemically
chemist
chemistry
cheque
  a bank cheque
chequered
  a chequered career
cherish
cheroot
cherry
  pl cherries
cherub
  pl cherubs,
   cherubim
chess
chest
chesterfield
chestnut
cheviot
chevron
chew
chic [shēk]

chicanery
chick
chicken
chicken out
  chickened out
  chickening out
chickenpox
chicory
chide
  chided
  chiding
chief
chiefly
chieftain
chiffon
chilblain
child
  pl children
childhood
childish
childlike
children *see* child
chill
chilli, chili
  chilli pepper:
  chili con carne
  pl chillies, chilies
chilly
  a chilly wind
chime
  chimed
  chiming
chimney
  pl chimneys
chimpanzee
chin
china
chinchilla
chink

chintz
chip
  chipped
  chipping
chipmunk
chipolata
chiropodist
chiropody
chirp
chirpy
  adv chirpily
chirrup
  chirruped
  chirruping
chisel
  chiselled
  chiselling
chit
chit-chat
chivalrous
chivalry
chive
chlorinate
  chlorinated
  chlorinating
chlorine
chloroform
chock-a-block
chock-full
chocolate
choice
choir
  a church choir:
  a children's choir
choke
  choked
  choking
cholera
choose

to choose a book
chose
He chose a book
chosen
He has chosen a book
choosing
chop
chopped
chopping
chopper
choppy
chopsticks
choral
chord
  a musical chord:
  the chord of a circle
chore
choreographer
choreography
chorister
chortle
  chortled
  chortling
chorus
  pl choruses
chose, chosen *see*
  choose
chow
christen
  christened
  christening
Christian
Christianity
Christmas
chromatic
chrome
chromium
chronic
  adv **chronically**

chronicle
chronicler
chronological
  adv
    chronologically
chronometer
chrysalis
chrysanthemum
chubby
chuck
chuckle
  chuckled
  chuckling
chum
chunk
church
  pl churches
churlish
churn
chute
  a rubbish chute:
  The child slid down
  the chute
chutney
  pl chutneys
cider
cigar
cigarette
cinder
cinema
cinnamon
cipher
circa
circle
  circled
  circling
circuit
circuitous
circular

circulate
  circulated
  circulating
circulation
circumference
circumlocution
circumspect
circumstances
circumstantial
circumstantiate
  circumstantiated
  circumstantiating
circumvent
circus
  pl circuses
cirrus clouds
cistern
citadel
citation
cite
  to cite as proof:
  to cite as a divorce
  co-respondent
cited
citing
citizen
citizenship
citric acid
citrus fruit
city
  pl cities
civic
civics
civil
  adv civilly
civilian
civility
  pl civilities
civilization,

-isation
civilize, -ise
 civilized
 civilizing
clad
claim
 claimed
 claiming
claimant
clairvoyance
clairvoyant
clamber
 clambered
 clambering
clammy
clamorous
clamour
clamp
clam up
 clammed up
 clamming up
clan
clandestine
 adv clandestinely
clang
clanger
clank
clannish
clap
 clapped
 clapping
claret
clarify
 clarified
 clarifying
clarinet
clarinettist
clarity
clash

pl clashes
class
 pl classes
classic
 adv classically
classical
classification
classify
 classified
 classifying
clatter
 clattered
 clattering
clause
claustrophobia
claustrophobic
claw
clay
clayey
claymore
clean
 cleaned
 cleaning
 cleaner
 cleanliness
 cleanness
 cleanse
 cleansed
 cleansing
clear
 cleared
 clearing
 clearance
 clearly
 clearness
 cleavage
cleave
cleaver
clef

cleft
cleg
clematis
clemency
clement
clench
clergy
clergyman
clerical
clerk
clever
cleverness
cliché
click
client
clientele
cliff
climate
climatic
climax
 pl climaxes
climb
climber
clinch
 pl clinches
cling
 clung
 clinging
clinic
clinical
 adv clinically
clink
clip
 clipped
 clipping
clipper
clique
cloak
cloche

36

clock
clockwise
clockwork
clod
clodhopper
clog
  clogged
  clogging
cloister
cloistered
close [klōs]
  adv closely
close [klōz]
  closed
  closing
closeness
closet
closet with
  closeted with
  closeting with
close-up
closure
clot
  clotted
  clotting
cloth
  pl cloths
  dish cloths
clothe
  clothed
  clothing
clothes
  bedclothes:
  children's clothes
clothing
cloud
cloudy
clove
cloven-hoofed

clover
clown
cloy
  cloyed
  cloying
club
  clubbed
  clubbing
cluck
clue
  pl clues
clump
clumsiness
clumsy
  adv clumsily
clung *see* cling
cluster
  clustered
  clustering
clutch
  pl clutches
clutter
  cluttered
  cluttering
coach
  pl coaches
coagulate
  coagulated
  coagulating
coal
coalesce
  coalesced
  coalescing
coalfield
coalition
coarse
  coarse sand: a coarse
  sense of humour
  adv coarsely

coarsen
  coarsened
  coarsening
coarseness
coast
coastal
coaster
coastguard
coat
  coated
  coating
coax
cob
cobalt
cobble
  cobbled
  cobbling
cobbler
cobra
cobweb
cocaine
cochineal
cock
cockade
cockatoo
cockatrice
cockerel
cocker spaniel
cockle
cockleshell
cockpit
cockroach
  pl cockroaches
cocksure
cocktail
cocky
  adv cockily
cocoa
coconut

cocoon
cod
coddle
  coddled
  coddling
code
codicil
co-driver
coeducation
coerce
  coerced
  coercing
coercion
coercive
coeval
coexist
coexistence
coffee
coffer
coffin
cog
cogency
cogent
cogitate
  cogitated
  cogitating
cognac
cognizance,
  -isance
cohere
  cohered
  cohering
coherence
coherent
cohesion
cohesive
cohort
coiffure
coil

coiled
coiling
coin
coined
coining
coinage
coincide
  coincided
  coinciding
coincidence
coincidental
coke
colander
cold
coldness
cole-slaw
colic
collaborate
  collaborated
  collaborating
collaboration
collaborator
collage
  The children made
  a collage
collapse
  collapsed
  collapsing
collapsible
collar
  collared
  collaring
collarbone
collate
  collated
  collating
collateral
collation
colleague

collect
collection
collective
  adv collectively
collector
college
  college and university
collegiate
collide
  collided
  colliding
collie
collier
colliery
  pl collieries
collision
colloquial
  adv colloquially
colloquialism
collusion
colon
colonel
colonial
colonist
colonization,
  -isation
colonize, -ise
  colonized
  colonizing
colonnade
colony
  pl colonies
colossal
colour
  coloured
  colouring
colourful
  adv colourfully
colourless

colt
column
coma
in a deep coma
comatose
comb
combat
combated
combating
combatant
combination
combine
combined
combining
combine
harvester
combustible
combustion
come
came
He came today
come
He has come
coming
comedian
comedy
pl comedies
comeliness
comely
comet
comfort
comfortable
adv comfortably
comic
comical
adv comically
coming *see* come
comma
a comma or a full stop

command
commandeer
commandeered
commandeering
commander
commandment
commando
pl commandoes
commemorate
commemorated
commemorating
commemoration
commence
commenced
commencing
commencement
commend
commendable
commendation
commensurate
comment
commentary
pl commentaries
commentator
commerce
commercial
adv commercially
commiserate
commiserated
commiserating
commiseration
commissariat
commission
commissioned
commissioning
commissionaire
*a cinema
commissionaire*
commissioner

*the High
Commissioner*
commit
committed
committing
commitment
committal
committee
commodious
commodity
pl commodities
commodore
common
commoner
commonplace
Commonwealth
commotion
communal
commune
communed
communing
communicate
communicated
communicating
communication
communicative
communion
communiqué
communism
communist
community
pl communities
commute
commuted
commuting
commuter
compact
companion
companionable

39

adv
   companionably
company
   pl companies
comparable
   adv comparably
comparative
   adv
   comparatively
compare
   compared
   comparing
comparison
compartment
compass
   *a compass to find
   the direction*
   pl compasses
   *The climbers
   carried compasses*
compasses
   *Use compasses to
   draw a circle*
compassion
compassionate
   adv compassion-
   ately
compatibility
compatible
   adv compatibly
compatriot
compel
   compelled
   compelling
compensate
   compensated
   compensating
compensation
compère

compete
competed
competing
competence
competent
competition
competitive
competitor
compilation
compile
   compiled
   compiling
compiler
complacency
complacent
complain
   complained
   complaining
complaint
complement
   *the complement of a
   verb: the complement
   of an angle: make up
   a full complement*
complementary
   *complementary
   angles:
   a complementary
   amount*
complete
   adv completely
   completed
   completing
   completeness
   completion
complex
   pl complexes
complexion
complexity

pl complexities
compliance
compliant
complicate
   complicated
   complicating
complication
complicity
complied *see*
   comply
compliment
   *a compliment to
   a beautiful woman*
complimentary
   *complimentary remark:
   complimentary ticket*
comply
   complied
   complying
component
compose
   composed
   composing
composite
composition
compositor
compost
composure
compound
comprehend
comprehensible
comprehension
comprehensive
   adv comprehen-
   sively
compress
compression
comprise
   comprised

40

comprising
compromise
  compromised
  compromising
compulsion
compulsive
  adv compulsively
compulsory
  adv compulsorily
compunction
computation
compute
  computed
  computing
computer
comrade
con
  conned
  conning
concave
conceal
  concealed
  concealing
concealment
concede
  conceded
  conceding
conceit
conceited
conceivable
  adv conceivably
conceive
  conceived
  conceiving
concentrate
  concentrated
  concentrating
concentration
concentric

concept
conception
concern
  concerning
concert
  a musical concert
concerted
concertina
concerto
  pl concertos
concession
conciliate
  conciliated
  conciliating
conciliation
conciliatory
concise
conciseness
conclude
  concluded
  concluding
conclusion
conclusive
  adv conclusively
concoct
concoction
concord
concourse
concrete
concur
  concurred
  concurring
concurrence
concurrent
concussion
condemn
  condemned
  condemning
condemnation

condensation
condense
  condensed
  condensing
condescend
condescending
condescension
condiment
condition
  conditioned
  conditioning
conditional
  adv conditionally
condole
  condoled
  condoling
condolences
condone
  condoned
  condoning
conducive
conduct
conduction
conductor
conductress
  pl conductresses
conduit
cone
coney see cony
confectioner
confectionery
confederacy
confederate
confederation
confer
  conferred
  conferring
conference
confess

confession
confetti
confidant
the king's trusted confidant
confidante
She was the queen's confidante
confide
confided
confiding
confidence
confident
confident of success
confidential
adv confidentially
confine
confined
confining
confinement
confines
confirm
confirmation
confiscate
confiscated
confiscating
confiscation
conflagration
conflict
confluence
conform
conformation
conformity
confound
confront
confrontation
confuse
confused
confusing

confusion
congeal
congealed
congealing
congenial
adv congenially
congenital
conger eel
congested
congestion
conglomeration
congratulate
congratulated
congratulating
congratulations
congratulatory
congregate
congregated
congregating
congregation
congregational
congress
pl congresses
congruent
congruity
congruous
conical
conifer
conjectural
conjecture
conjectured
conjecturing
conjugal
conjugate
conjugated
conjugating
conjugation
conjunction
conjunctivitis

conjure
conjured
conjuring
conjuror
connect
connection
conned *see* con
connive at
connived at
conniving at
connoisseur
connotation
conquer
conquered
conquering
conqueror
conquest
conscience
a bad conscience
conscientious
a conscientious worker
conscientiousness
conscious
*Is the patient conscious now?:
a conscious decision:
conscious of his disability*

consciousness
conscript
conscription
consecrate
consecrated
consecrating
consecration
consecutive
adv consecutively
consensus
consent

consequence
consequent
consequential
consequently
conservation
conservationist
conservative
conservatory
  pl conservatories
conserve
  conserved
  conserving
consider
  considered
  considering
considerable
  adv considerably
considerate
  adv considerately
consideration
consign
consignment
consist
consistency
consistent
consolation
console
  consoled
  consoling
consolidate
  consolidated
  consolidating
consolidation
consonant
'consort
  the Queen's consort
con'sort
  to consort with
  criminals

conspicuous
conspiracy
  pl conspiracies
conspirator
conspire
  conspired
  conspiring
constable
constabulary
constancy
constant
constellation
consternation
constipation
constituency
  pl constituencies
constituent
constitute
  constituted
  constituting
constitutional
  adv
    constitutionally
constrain
constraint
constrict
construct
construction
constructive
  adv constructively
consul
  He is British consul
  in Spain
consulate
consult
consultant
consultation
consume
  consumed

consuming
consumer
consummate
  consummated
  consummating
consumption
contact
contagious
contain
  contained
  containing
container
contaminate
  contaminated
  contaminating
contamination
contemplate
  contemplated
  contemplating
contemplation
contemporary
contempt
contemptible
  adv contemptibly
contemptuous
contend
content
contented
contention
contentious
contentment
contents
contest
contestant
context
continent
continental
contingency
  pl contingencies

contingent
continual

in continual pain:
There have been
continual attacks
on his life

adv continually
continuance
continuation
continue
  continued
  continuing
continuity
continuous

a continuous line
of cars

adv continuously
contort
contortion
contortionist
contour
contraband
contraception
contraceptive
contract
contraction
contractor
contradict
contradiction
contradictory
contralto
  pl contraltos
contraption
contrary
contrast
contravene
  contravened
  contravening
contravention

contretemps
contribute
  contributed
  contributing
contribution
contributor
contrite
  adv contritely
contrition
contrivance
contrive
  contrived
  contriving
control
  controlled
  controlling
  controller
  controls
controversial
  adv
    controversially
controversy
  pl controversies
conundrum
conurbation
convalesce
  convalesced
  convalescing
  convalescence
convalescent
convection
convector
convene
  convened
  convening
  convener
convenience
convenient
convent

convention
conventional
  adv
    conventionally
converge
  converged
  converging
convergence
convergent
conversation
conversational
  adv conversation-
    ally
converse
  conversed
  conversing
conversion
convert
convertible
convex
convey
  conveyed
  conveying
conveyance
conveyor belt
convict
conviction
convince
  convinced
  convincing
convivial
  adv convivially
conviviality
convocation
convolvulus
convoy
  convoyed
  convoying
convulse

convulsed
convulsing
convulsion
convulsive
  adv convulsively
cony, coney
coo
  cooed
  cooing
cook
cooker
cookery
cooking
cool
  adv **coolly**
coolness
coop
  a chicken coop
cooper
co-operate
  co-operated
  co-operating
co-operation
co-operative
  adv co-
    operatively
co-opt
  co-opted
  co-opting
coop up
  cooped up
  cooping up
co-ordinate
  co-ordinated
  co-ordinating
co-ordination
coot
cope
  coped

coping
coping-stone
copious
copper
copperplate
coppice
copra
copse
copy
  pl copies
  copied
  copying
copyright
coquette
coquettish
coracle
coral
  a coral reef:
  a necklace of coral
cord
  the cord of a
  dressing-gown: spinal
  cord: vocal cords
cordial
  adv cordially
cordiality
cordite
cordon
cordon bleu
cordon off
  cordoned off
  cordoning off
corduroy
core
  cored
  coring
co-respondent
  the co-respondent in
  a divorce case

corgi
  pl corgis
cork
corkscrew
corm
cormorant
corn
cornea
  pl corneas
corner
  cornered
  cornering
corner-stone
cornet
  He plays the cornet:
  ice-cream cornet
cornflour
  to thicken the sauce
  with cornflour
cornflower
  a pretty blue
  cornflower
cornice
corollary
  pl corollaries
coronary
  pl coronaries
coronation
coroner
coronet
  a baron's coronet
corporal
corporate
corporation
corps [kör]
  corps of an army:
  corps de ballet
  pl corps
corpse

45

dead as a corpse
pl corpses
corpulence
corpulent
corpuscle
corral
  cattle in the corral:
  a corral of wagons
correct
correction
corrective
correspond
correspondence
correspondent
  a letter from a
  regular correspondent
corridor
corrigendum
  pl corrigenda
corroborate
  corroborated
  corroborating
  corroboration
  corroborative
corrode
  corroded
  corroding
corrosion
corrosive
corrugated
corrupt
corruptible
corruption
corset
cortège
cosh
  pl coshes
cosmetic
cosmic

cosmonaut
cosmopolitan
cosset
  cosseted
  cosseting
cost
  cost
  That coat cost £30:
  That has cost him
  his life
costed
  Have you costed
  the research project?
costing
costermonger
costliness
costly
costume
cosy
  adv cosily
cot
coterie
cottage
cottager
cotton
cottonwool
couch
  pl couches
couch grass
couchant
cougar
cough
could *see* can
coulomb
council
  the town council
councillor
  a town councillor
counsel

He was her counsel
in the divorce case
counsel
  to counsel him to stay
  counselled
  counselling
counsellor
  a marriage guidance
  counsellor
count
countenance
  countenanced
  countenancing
counter
  countered
  countering
counteract
counterfeit
counterfoil
countermand
counterpane
counterpart
countersign
countess
  pl countesses
countless
country
  pl countries
countryside
county
  pl counties
coup
  The president was
  killed in the coup
couple
  coupled
  coupling
couplet
coupon

46

courage
courageous
courgette
courier
course

the course of the river: in the course of time: in due course

coursing
court
courteous
courtesy

He behaved with politeness and courtesy

courtier
courtly
court-martial
  pl courts-martial
courtship
courtyard
cousin
cove
coven
covenant
covenanter
cover
  covered
  covering
coverage
coverlet
covert
covet
  coveted
  coveting
covetous
covetousness
covey
  pl coveys

coward
cowardice
cowardly
cowboy
cowed
cower
  cowered
  cowering
cowherd
cowl
cowslip
cox
coxcomb
coxswain
coy
coyote
crab
crabbed
crack
cracker
crackle
  crackled
  crackling
cradle
  cradled
  cradling
craft
craftsman
crafty
  adv craftily
crag
craggy
cram
  crammed
  cramming
cramp
cramped
crampon
cranberry

  pl cranberries
crane
crank
cranky
cranny
  pl crannies
crape *see* crêpe
crash
  pl crashes
crass
crate
crater
cravat
crave
  craved
  craving
crawl
crayfish
crayon
craze
crazy
  adv crazily
creak

the creak of the stairs: The beams began to creak

cream
  creamed
  creaming
creamy
crease
  creased
  creasing
create
  created
  creating
creation
creative
creator

creature
crèche
credentials
credibility
credible
  adv credibly
credit
  credited
  crediting
creditable
creditor
credulity
credulous
creed
creek
  fishing-boats in the creek: canoeing in the creek
creep
  crept
  creeping
creeper
cremate
  cremated
  cremating
cremation
crematorium
creosote
crêpe, crape
crept *see* creep
crescent
cress
crest
crestfallen
crevasse
  a crevasse in the ice
crevice
  a crevice in the rock
crew

crewcut
crib
  cribbed
  cribbing
cribbage
crick
cricket
cricketer
cried *see* cry
crier
cries *see* cry
crime
criminal
  adv criminally
crimson
cringe
  cringed
  cringing
crinkle
  crinkled
  crinkling
crinkly
crinoline
cripple
  crippled
  crippling
crisis
  pl crises
crisp
crispy
criss-cross
criterion
  pl criteria
critic
critical
  adv critically
criticism
criticize, -ise
  criticized

criticizing
croak
croaky
crochet ['krōshā]
  to crochet a shawl
  crocheted
  crocheting
crock
crockery
crocodile
crocus
  pl crocuses
croft
crofter
crone
crony
  pl cronies
crook
crooked
crookedness
croon
  crooned
  crooning
crooner
crop
  cropped
  cropping
cropper
croquet
cross
  pl crosses
  crossed
  crossing
cross-examine
  cross-examined
  cross-examining
crossing
crossness
crossroads

48

cross-section
crotchet
   a musical crotchet
crotchety
crouch
croup
croupier
crow
   crowed, (*old*)
   crew
   The baby crowed:
   The cock crew
   crowing
crowbar
crowd
crowded
crown
crucial
   adv **crucially**
crucible
crucifix
   pl crucifixes
crucifixion
crucify
   crucified
   crucifying
crude
   adv crudely
crudeness
crudity
cruel
   adv **cruelly**
cruelty
cruise
   cruised
   cruising
cruiser
crumb
crumble

crumbled
crumbling
crumbly
crumpet
crumple
   crumpled
   crumpling
crunch
crusade
crusader
crush
crust
crustacean
crusty
crutch
   pl crutches
crux
cry
   pl cries
   cried
   crying
crypt
cryptic
   adv cryptically
crystal
crystalline
crystallization,
   -isation
crystallize, -ise
   crystallized
   crystallizing
cub
cube
cubic
cubicle
cuckoo
   pl cuckoos
cucumber
cud

cuddle
   cuddled
   cuddling
cudgel
cue
   a cue in billiards:
   The actor missed
   his cue
cuff
   pl cuffs
cufflinks
cuisine
cul-de-sac
culinary
cull
culminate
   culminated
   culminating
culmination
culpable
culprit
cult
cultivate
   cultivated
   cultivating
cultivation
culture
cultured
cumbersome
cummerbund
cumulative
cumulus
cunning
cup
   cupped
   cupping
cupboard
cupful
   pl cupfuls

cupidity
cupola
cup-tie
cur
curable
curate
curator
curb
*to act as a curb on
his extravagances:
Curb your desires!*
curd
curdle
curdled
curdling
cure
cured
curing
curfew
curio
pl curios
curiosity
pl curiosities
curious
curl
curlew
curling
curly
currant
*currants and sultanas:
black and red currants*
currency
pl currencies
current
*a current of air:
an electric current:
the current financial
year: a current
account: That rumour
is current*

curriculum
pl curricula,
curriculums
curriculum vitae
pl curricula vitae
curry
pl curries
curried
currying
curse
cursed
cursing
cursory
adv cursorily
curt
curtail
curtailed
curtailing
curtailment
curtain
curtness
curtsy, curtsey
*She made a curtsy
to the queen*
pl curtsies,
curtseys
curtsied
curtsying,
curtseying
curvature
curve
curved
curving
cushion
cushioned
cushioning
cushy
custard
custodian

custody
custom
customary
adv customarily
customer
cut
cut
cutting
cute
adv cutely
cuteness
cuticle
cutlass
pl cutlasses
cutlery
cutlet
cutting
cuttlefish
cut-up
cyanide
cycle
cycled
cycling
cyclist
cyclone
cygnet
a swan and her cygnet
cylinder
cylindrical
adv cylindrically
cymbal
He plays the cymbals
cynic
cynical
adv cynically
cynicism
cynosure
cypress
pl cypresses

cyst
cystitis
czar *see* tsar

D

dab
  dabbed
  dabbing
dabble
  dabbled
  dabbling
dachshund
dad
daddy
  pl daddies
dado
  pl dadoes, dados
daffodil
daft
dagger
dahlia
daily
  pl dailies
daintiness
dainty
  adv daintily
dairy
  milk from the dairy
  pl dairies
dais
  pl daises
daisy
  pl daisies
dale
dalliance
dally
  dallied
  dallying

dam
  to dam a river
  dammed
  He dammed up the river
  damming
damage
  damaged
  damaging
damask
dame
dammed *see* dam
damn
  to damn a soul:
  Damn! I've dropped it
  damned
  a damned soul:
  that damned dog
  damning
damnable
damnation
damned *see* damn
damp
dampen
  dampened
  dampening
damper
dampness
damsel
damson
dance
  danced
  dancing
dancer
dandelion
dandruff
danger
dangerous

dangle
  dangled
  dangling
Danish
dank
dapper
dappled
dare
  dared
  daring
daredevil
dark
darken
  darkened
  darkening
darkness
darling
darn
dart
dartboard
dash
  pl dashes
dashing
dastardly
data
  sing datum
date
  dated
  dating
datum *see* data
daub
  daubed
  daubing
daughter
daughter-in-law
  pl daughters-in-law
daunt
dauntless

dawdle
  dawdled
  dawdling
dawn
day
daydream
daze
  dazed
  dazing
dazzle
  dazzled
  dazzling
deacon
deaconess
  pl deaconesses
dead
deaden
  deadened
  deadening
deadline
deadliness
deadly
deadness
deaf
deafen
  deafened
  deafening
deafness
deal
  dealt
  dealing
dealer
dean
dear
  *a dear friend: The
  shoes are too dear*
dearly
dearness
dearth

death
deathly
debar
  debarred
  debarring
debase
  debased
  debasing
  debasement
debatable
debate
  debated
  debating
debauched
debauchery
debilitate
  debilitated
  debilitating
debility
debit
  debited
  debiting
debonair
débris, debris
debt
debtor
début, debut
debutante
decade
decadence
decadent
decanter
decapitate
  decapitated
  decapitating
decathlon
decay
  decayed
  decaying

decease
deceased
deceit
deceitful
  adv deceitfully
deceive
  deceived
  deceiving
deceiver
decelerate
  decelerated
  decelerating
December
decency
decent
deception
deceptive
  adv deceptively
decibel
decide
  decided
  deciding
decidedly
deciduous
decimal
decimalization,
  -isation
decimalize, -ise
  decimalized
  decimalizing
decimate
  decimated
  decimating
decipher
  deciphered
  deciphering
decision
decisive
  adv decisively

deck
declaim
  declaimed
  declaiming
declamation
declamatory
declaration
declare
  declared
  declaring
decline
  declined
  declining
decode
  decoded
  decoding
decompose
  decomposed
  decomposing
decomposition
décor, decor
decorate
  decorated
  decorating
decoration
decorative
  adv decoratively
decorator
decorous
decorum
decoy
  decoyed
  decoying
decrease
  decreased
  decreasing
decree
  decreed
  decreeing

decrepit
decry
  to decry modern youth
  decried
  decrying
dedicate
  dedicated
  dedicating
dedication
deduce
  deduced
  deducing
deduct
deduction
deed
deep
deepen
  deepened
  deepening
deer
  He shot a deer
  pl deer
deface
  defaced
  defacing
defacement
defamation
defamatory
defame
  defamed
  defaming
default
defaulter
defeat
  defeated
  defeating
defect
defection
defective

defence
defenceless
defend
defendant
defensible
defensive
  adv defensively
defer
  deferred
  deferring
deference
deferential
  adv deferentially
defiance
defiant
deficiency
  pl deficiencies
deficient
deficit
defied *see* defy
defile
  defiled
  defiling
defilement
define
  defined
  defining
definite
  adv **definitely**
definition
definitive
  adv definitively
deflate
  deflated
  deflating
deflation
deflect
deflection
deform

deformed
deformity
  pl deformities
defraud
defray
  defrayed
  defraying
defrost
deft
defunct
defy
  defied
  defying
degenerate
  degenerated
  degenerating
degenerative
degradation
degrade
  degraded
  degrading
degree
dehydrate
  dehydrated
  dehydrating
  dehydration
deify
  deified
  deifying
deign
  deigned
  deigning
deity
  pl deities
dejected
dejection
delay
  delayed
  delaying

delectable
  adv delectably
delegate
  delegated
  delegating
  delegation
delete
  deleted
  deleting
deleterious
deletion
deliberate
  adv deliberately
  deliberated
  deliberating
  deliberation
delicacy
  pl delicacies
delicate
  adv delicately
delicatessen
delicious
delight
  delighted
  delightful
  adv delightfully
delinquency
delinquent
delirious
delirium
deliver
  delivered
  delivering
deliverance
delivery
  pl deliveries
dell
delphinium
delta

delude
  deluded
  deluding
deluge
  deluged
  deluging
delusion
  *He's under
  the delusion that
  he's Napoleon*
delve
  delved
  delving
demand
demean
  demeaned
  demeaning
demeanour
demented
demise
demo
demob
  demobbed
  demobbing
demobilization,
  -isation
demobilize, -ise
  demobilized
  demobilizing
democracy
  pl democracies
democrat
democratic
  adv
    democratically
demolish
demolition
demon
demonstrable

adv demonstrably
demonstrate
demonstrated
demonstrating
demonstration
demonstrative
demonstrator
demoralize, -ise
demoralized
demoralizing
demote
demoted
demoting
demotion
demur
demurred
demurring
demure
adv demurely
demureness
den
denial
denied *see* deny
denier
denigrate
denigrated
denigrating
denim
denizen
denomination
denominational
denominator
denote
denoted
denoting
denounce
denounced
denouncing
dénouement

dense
adv densely
denseness
density
pl densities
dent
dental
dentist
dentistry
denture
denudation
denude
denuded
denuding
denunciation
deny
denied
denying
deodorant
depart
department
departure
depend
dependable
dependant
His wife and children
are his dependants
dependence
dependent
His wife is dependent
on him
depict
deplete
depleted
depleting
depletion
deplorable
adv deplorably
deplore

deplored
deploring
deploy
deployed
deploying
depopulated
deport
deportation
deportment
depose
deposed
deposing
deposit
deposition
depository
pl depositories
depot, depôt
depraved
depravity
deprecate
to deprecate
her behaviour
deprecated
deprecating
deprecation
depreciate
The pound will
depreciate
depreciated
depreciating
depreciation
depredation
depress
depression
deprivation
deprive
deprived
depriving
depth

deputation
deputize, -ise
  deputized
  deputizing
deputy
  pl deputies
derail
  derailed
  derailing
derailment
deranged
derangement
derelict
dereliction
deride
  derided
  deriding
derision
derisive
  adv derisively
derivation
derivative
derive
  derived
  deriving
dermatitis
dermatologist
dermatology
derogatory
  adv derogatorily
derrick
descant
descend
  descended
  descending
descendant
  He is a descendant
  of Queen Victoria
descendent

a descendent slope
descent
describe
  described
  describing
description
descriptive
descry
  to descry a ship
  at sea
  descried
  descrying
desecrate
  desecrated
  desecrating
  desecration
de'sert
  to desert from
  the army: to desert
  one's family
'desert
  a desert island
deserter
desertion
deserve
  deserved
  deserving
  deservedly
desiccate
  desiccated
  desiccating
desiccation
design
  designed
  designing
designate
  designated
  designating
designation

desirability
desirable
  adv desirably
desire
  desired
  desiring
desirous
desist
desk
desolate
  desolated
  desolation
despair
  despaired
  despairing
despatch *see*
  dispatch
desperado
  pl desperadoes,
    desperados
desperate
  adv desperately
desperation
despicable
  adv despicably
despise
  despised
  despising
despite
despoil
  despoiled
  despoiling
despoliation
despondency
despondent
despot
despotic
  adv despotically
despotism

dessert
  the dessert course
destination
destined
destiny
destitute
destroy
  destroyed
  destroying
destroyer
destructible
destruction
destructive
desultory
  adv desultorily
detach
  detached
  detaching
detachable
detachment
detail
  detailed
  detailing
detain
  detained
  detaining
detect
detection
detective
détente
detention
deter
  deterred
  deterring
detergent
deteriorate
  deteriorated
  deteriorating
  deterioration

determination
determine
  determined
  determining
deterrent
detest
detestable
  adv detestably
detestation
detonate
  detonated
  detonating
  detonator
detour
detract
detraction
detriment
detrimental
deuce
devastate
  devastated
  devastating
  devastation
develop
  developed
  developing
  developer
development
deviate
  deviated
  deviating
  deviation
device
  a device
  for boring holes
devil
devilish
devilry
devious

devise
  to devise a plan
  devised
  devising
devoid
devolution
  the devolution of
  power from central
  government
devolve
  devolved
  devolving
devote
  devoted
  devoting
devotee
devotion
devour
devout
devoutness
dew
  the morning dew
dewy
dexterity
dexterous,
  dextrous
diabetes
diabetic
diabolic
diabolical
  adv diabolically
diadem
diagnose
  diagnosed
  diagnosing
diagnosis
  pl diagnoses
diagnostic
diagonal

adv diagonally
diagram
diagrammatic
dial
 dialled
 dialling
dialect
dialectal
dialogue
diameter
diametric
 adv diametrically
diamond
diaphragm
diarrhoea
diary
 *Make a note
 in your diary*
 pl diaries
diatribe
dice
dictate
 dictated
 dictating
dictation
dictator
dictatorial
 adv dictatorially
diction
dictionary
 pl dictionaries
did *see* do
die
 to die young
 died
 He died young
 dying
 dying young
diesel

diet
dietetic
differ
 differed
 differing
difference
different
differentiate
 differentiated
 differentiating
 differentiation
difficult
difficulty
 pl difficulties
diffidence
diffident
diffuse
dig
 dug
 digging
digest
digestible
digestion
digestive
digger
digit
digital
digitalis
dignified
dignitary
 pl dignitaries
dignity
digress
digression
dike, dyke
dilapidated
dilatation
dilate
 dilated

dilating
dilatory
dilemma
dilettante
diligence
diligent
dilly-dally
 dilly-dallied
 dilly-dallying
dilute
 diluted
 diluting
dilution
dim
 dimmed
 dimming
dimension
dimensional
diminish
diminution
diminutive
dimness
dimple
din
 dinned
 dinning
dine
 dined
 dining
dinghy
 a sailing dinghy
 pl dinghies
dinginess
dingy
 dark and dingy
dinner
dinosaur
dint
diocesan

diocese
dip
  dipped
  dipping
diphtheria
diphthong
diploma
  pl diplomas
diplomacy
diplomat
diplomatic
  adv
    diplomatically
dire
direct
  directed
  directing
direction
directly
directness
director
directory
  pl directories
dirge
dirt
dirtiness
dirty
  adv dirtily
  dirtied
  dirtying
disability
  pl disabilities
disable
  disabled
  disabling
disablement
disabuse
  disabused
  disabusing

disadvantage
disadvantaged
disadvantageous
disaffected
disagree
  disagreed
  disagreeing
disagreeable
  adv disagreeably
disagreement
disallow
disappear
  disappeared
  disappearing
disappearance
disappoint
  disappointed
  disappointment
disapproval
disapprove
  disapproved
  disapproving
disarm
  disarming
disarrange
  disarranged
  disarranging
disarrangement
disarray
disaster
disastrous
disband
disbelief
  He looked at me
  in disbelief
disbelieve
  to disbelieve a story
  disbelieved
  disbelieving

disburse
disc, disk
discard
discern
discernible
  adv discernibly
discerning
discernment
discharge
  discharged
  discharging
disciple
disciplinarian
disciplinary
discipline
disclaim
disclaimer
disclose
  disclosed
  disclosing
disclosure
disco
discoloration,
  discolouration
discolour
  discoloured
  discolouring
discomfiture
discomfort
disconcert
disconnect
disconnection
disconsolate
  adv
    disconsolately
discontent
discontented
discontentment
discontinue

59

discontinued
discontinuing
discord
discordant
discothèque
discount
discourage
discouraged
discouraging
discouragement
discourse
discoursed
discoursing
discourteous
discover
discovered
discovering
discoverer
discovery
　pl discoveries
discredit
discredited
discrediting
discreditable
discreet
discrepancy
　pl discrepancies
discretion
discriminate
discriminated
discriminating
discrimination
discus
　He throws the discus
discuss
　to discuss a problem
discussion
disdain
disdained

disdaining
disdainful
　adv disdainfully
disease
diseased
disembark
disembarkation
disembodied
disengage
disengaged
disengaging
disentangle
disentangled
disentangling
disfavour
disfigure
disfigured
disfiguring
disfigurement
disgorge
disgorged
disgorging
disgrace
disgraced
disgracing
disgraceful
　adv disgracefully
disgruntled
disguise
disguised
disguising
disgust
disgusted
dish
　pl dishes
dishearten
disheartened
disheartening
dishevelled

dishonest
dishonesty
dishonour
dishonourable
　adv
　dishonourably
disillusion
disillusioned
disillusioning
disillusionment
disinclined
disinfect
disinfectant
disinherit
disinherited
disinheriting
disintegrate
disintegrated
disintegrating
disintegration
disinterested
disjointed
disk *see* disc
dislike
disliked
disliking
dislocate
dislocated
dislocating
dislocation
dislodge
dislodged
dislodging
disloyal
　adv disloyally
disloyalty
dismal
　adv dismally
dismantle

dismantled
dismantling
dismay
  dismayed
  dismaying
dismember
  dismembered
  dismembering
dismemberment
dismiss
  dismissal
dismount
disobedience
disobedient
disobey
  disobeyed
  disobeying
disobliging
disorder
  disordered
  disorderliness
  disorderly
disown
disparage
  disparaged
  disparaging
disparagement
disparity
  pl disparities
dispassionate
  adv
    dispassionately
dispatch,
  despatch
  pls dispatches,
    despatches
dispel
  dispelled
  dispelling

dispensable
dispensary
  pl dispensaries
dispensation
dispense
  dispensed
  dispensing
  dispenser
dispersal
disperse
  dispersed
  dispersing
dispirited
displace
  displaced
  displacing
displacement
display
  displayed
  displaying
displease
  displeased
  displeasing
displeasure
disposable
disposal
dispose
  disposed
  disposing
disposition
dispossess
disproportionate
  adv disproportion-
    ately
disprove
disputable
disputation
dispute
  disputed

disputing
disqualification
disqualify
  disqualified
  disqualifying
disquiet
  disquieting
disregard
disrepair
disreputable
  adv disreputably
disrepute
disrespect
disrespectful
  adv
    disrespectfully
disrupt
disruption
disruptive
dissatisfaction
dissatisfy
  dissatisfied
  dissatisfying
dissect
dissemble
  dissembled
  dissembling
disseminate
  disseminated
  disseminating
dissemination
dissension
dissent
  dissented
  dissenting
dissenter
dissertation
disservice
dissimilar

dissimilarity
  pl dissimilarities
dissimulate
  dissimulated
  dissimulating
dissipate
  dissipated
  dissipating
dissipation
dissociate
  dissociated
  dissociating
dissociation
dissolute
dissolution
dissolve
  dissolved
  dissolving
dissonance
dissonant
dissuade
  dissuaded
  dissuading
distaff
distance
distant
distaste
distasteful
  adv distastefully
distemper
distend
distension
distil
  distilled
  distilling
distillation
distillery
  pl distilleries
distinct

distinction
distinctive
distinguish
distinguished
distort
distortion
distract
distraction
distraught
distress
distribute
  distributed
  distributing
distribution
district
distrust
distrustful
  adv distrustfully
disturb
disturbance
disuse
  disused
ditch
  pl ditches
dither
  dithered
  dithering
ditto
ditty
  pl ditties
divan
dive
  dived
  diving
diver
diverge
  diverged
  diverging
divergence

divergent
diverse
diversify
  diversified
  diversifying
diversion
diversity
divert
divest
divide
  divided
  dividing
dividend
divination
divine
  divined
  divining
divinity
  pl divinities
divisibility
divisible
division
divisional
divisor
divorce
  divorced
  divorcing
divorcee
divulge
  divulged
  divulging
dizziness
dizzy
do
  does, do
  did
  He did it
  done
  He has done it

doing
docile
  adv docilely
docility
dock
docker
docket
doctor
  doctored
  doctoring
doctrinal
doctrine
document
documentary
  pl documentaries
dodder
doddery
dodge
  dodged
  dodging
dodo
  pl dodos, dodoes
doe
  a buck and a doe
doer
does *see* do
doff
dog
  dogged
  dogging
dogged
  adv doggedly
doggerel
dogma
dogmatic
  adv dogmatically
doily, doyley
  a doily for a cake
doing *see* do

doldrums
dole
doleful
  adv dolefully
dolefulness
dole out
  doled out
  doling out
dollar
dolly
  a child's dolly:
  a dolly bird
  pl dollies
dolphin
dolt
domain
dome
domestic
  adv domestically
domesticated
domesticity
domicile
dominance
dominant
dominate
  dominated
  dominating
domination
domineer
  domineered
  domineering
dominion
domino
  pl dominoes
don
  donned
  donning
donate
  donated

donating
donation
done *see* do
donkey
  pl donkeys
donor
don't
  = do not
doom
doomed
door
doorway
dope
  doped
  doping
dormant
dormer window
dormitory
  pl dormitories
dormouse
  pl dormice
dorsal
dose
  dosed
  dosing
doss down
dossier
dot
dotage
dote on
  doted on
  doting on
dotted
double
  adv doubly
  doubled
  doubling
doublet
doubt

doubted
doubting
doubtful
  adv doubtfully
doubtless
dough
  dough for bread
doughnut
dove
dovecote
dovetail
  dovetailed
  dovetailing
dowdy
  adv dowdily
down
downfall
downstairs
downtrodden
downwards
dowry
  pl dowries
doyley *see* doily
doze
  dozed
  dozing
dozen
drab
draft
  a rough draft:
  to draft a plan
drag
  dragged
  dragging
dragon
  St George and
  the dragon
dragonfly
  pl dragonflies

dragoon
  the dragoon guards:
  Did he dragoon you
  into going?
dragooned
dragooning
drain
drainage
drake
drama
  pl dramas
dramatic
  adv dramatically
dramatist
dramatization,
  -isation
dramatize, -ise
  dramatized
  dramatizing
drank *see* drink
drape
  draped
  draping
draper
drapery
drastic
  adv **drastically**
draught
  a cold draught:
  a draught of ale
draughtsman
draughty
draw
  drew
  He drew a sketch
  drawn
  He has drawn a sketch
  drawing
  drawer

drawl
drawn *see* draw
dread
dreadful
  adv dreadfully
dreadfulness
dream
  dreamed,
  dreamt
  dreaming
dreamy
  adv dreamily
dreary
  adv drearily
dredge
  dredged
  dredging
dredger
dregs
drench
dress
  pl dresses
  dressed
  dressing
  dresser
drew *see* draw
drey
  pl dreys
dribble
  dribbled
  dribbling
dried *see* dry
drift
driftwood
drill
drily *see* dry
drink
  drank
  He drank some water

drunk
*He has drunk
some water*

drinking

drip
dripped
dripping

drip-dry
drip-dried
drip-drying

drive
drove
He drove her car
driven
He has driven her car
driving

drivel
drivelled
drivelling

driven *see* drive

driver

drizzle
drizzled
drizzling

drizzly

droll

dromedary
pl dromedaries

drone
droned
droning

drool
drooled
drooling

droop
drooped
drooping

drop
dropped

dropping
droplet
droppings
dross
drought
drove *see* drive
drove
drown
drowsy
adv drowsily

drudge
drudged
drudging
drudgery

drug
drugged
drugging
druggist

drum
drummed
drumming
drummer
drumstick

drunk *see* drink
drunkard
drunken
drunkenness

dry
adv dryly, drily
dried
drying
dryad
dry-clean
dry-cleaned
dry-cleaning

dual
*a dual purpose:
a dual carriageway*

dub

dubbed
dubbing
dubiety
dubious
ducal
duchess
pl duchesses
duchy
pl duchies
duck
ducked
ducking
duck
ducks and drakes
duckling
duct
dud
dudgeon
in high dudgeon
due
*Your account is due:
Go due south: death
due to starvation*
duel
They fought a duel
duellist
dues
duet
duffel-coat,
duffle coat
dug *see* dig
dug-out
duke
dukedom
dulcet
dulcimer
dull
adv dully
He spoke dully

and boringly
dullness
duly
He duly arrived
dumb
adv **dumbly**
dumbfound
dumbness
dummy
pl **dummies**
dump
dumpling
dumpy
dun
dunned
dunning
dunce
dune
dung
dungarees
dungeon
jailed in a dungeon
dupe
duped
duping
duplicate
duplicated
duplicating
duplication
duplicity
durable
adv **durably**
duration
duress
during
dusk
dusky
dust
duster
66

dusty
Dutch
dutiable
dutiful
adv **dutifully**
duty
pl **duties**
dux
the dux of the school
dwarf
pl **dwarfs,**
   dwarves
dwarfed
dwarfing
dwell
dwelled, dwelt
dwelling
dwindle
dwindled
dwindling
dye
to dye a dress red
dyed
She dyed her dress
dyeing
dyeing a dress red
dying *see* **die**
dyke *see* **dike**
dynamic
adv **dynamically**
dynamite
dynamo
pl **dynamos**
dynastic
dynasty
pl **dynasties**
dysentery
dyspepsia
dyspeptic

E

each
eager
eagerness
eagle
ear
eardrum
earl
earliness
early
compar **earlier**
superl **earliest**
adv **early**
earmark
earn
earnest
earnings
earth
earthenware
earthly
in this earthly life:
no earthly use
earthquake
earthy
an earthy sense of
humour: These
potatoes are very
earthy
earwig
ease
eased
easing
easel
easier, easiest *see*
   easy
east
Easter
easterly

an easterly wind
eastern
   eastern customs
eastward
eastwards
easy
   compar **easier**
   superl **easiest**
   adv **easily**
eat
   ate
   He ate a cake
   eaten
   He has eaten a cake
   eating
eatable
eaten *see* **eat**
eaves
eavesdrop
   eavesdropped
   eavesdropping
ebb
ebony
ebullience
ebullient
eccentric
eccentricity
   pl **eccentricities**
ecclesiastic
ecclesiastical
echo
   pl **echoes**
eclipse
   an eclipse of the sun:
   to eclipse his glory
   eclipsed
   eclipsing
ecological
   adv **ecologically**

ecologist
ecology
economic
   the country's
   economic future:
   an economic rent
   adv **economically**
economical
   economical use of
   supplies: He is
   extravagant; she is
   economical
   adv **economically**
economics
economist
economize, -ise
   economized
   economizing
economy
   pl **economies**
ecstasy
   pl **ecstasies**
ecstatic
   adv **ecstatically**
eczema
eddy
   pl **eddies**
edge
   edged
   edging
edgeways
edgy
   adv **edgily**
edible
edict
edification
edifice
edify
   edified

edifying
edit
   edited
   editing
edition
   a new edition of his
   book: the evening
   edition of the
   newspaper
editor
editorial
   adv **editorially**
educate
   educated
   educating
education
educational
   adv **educationally**
eel
eerie
   an eerie silence:
   a dark eerie house
   adv **eerily**
eeriness
efface
   effaced
   effacing
effect
   the effect of the
   drug: the effect of
   the new lighting:
   The new law is not yet
   in effect: goods and
   effects: to effect
   a reconciliation
   effected
   effecting
effective
   adv **effectively**

effectual
  adv effectually
effeminate
  adv effeminately
effervesce
  effervesced
  effervescing
effervescence
effervescent
efficacious
efficacy
efficiency
efficient
effigy
  pl effigies
effluent
  The factory's effluent
  caused disease
effort
effortless
effrontery
effusive
  adv effusively
egg
egg on
  egged on
  egging on
egoism
egoist
egoistic
  adv egoistically
egotism
egotist
egotistic
  adv egotistically
eiderdown
eider duck
eight
eighteen

eighteenth
eighth
eightieth
eighty
either
ejaculate
  ejaculated
  ejaculating
  ejaculation
eject
ejection
ejector
eke out
  eked out
  eking out
elaborate
  elaborated
  elaborating
élan
elapse
  elapsed
  elapsing
elastic
elasticity
elated
elation
elbow
  pl elbows
  elbowed
  elbowing
elder
  the elder of the
  (two) brothers
elderberry
  pl elderberries
elderly
eldest
  the eldest of
  four brothers

elect
election
electioneer
  electioneered
  electioneering
electorate
electric
  adv electrically
electrical
  adv electrically
electrician
electricity
electrify
  electrified
  electrifying
electrocute
  electrocuted
  electrocuting
electrode
electron
electronic
  adv electronically
electronics
elegance
elegant
elegy
  pl elegies
element
elementary
elephant
elevate
  elevated
  elevating
elevation
elevator
eleven
elevenses
eleventh
elf

pl elves
elfin
elfish
elicit
  to elicit information
elicited
eliciting
eligibility
eligible
  an eligible bachelor:
  eligible for the job
eliminate
  eliminated
  eliminating
elimination
élite
elixir
elk
ellipse
  a geometrical ellipse
  pl ellipses
elliptical
  adv elliptically
elm
elocution
elongate
  elongated
  elongating
elongation
elope
  eloped
  eloping
elopement
eloquence
eloquent
else
elsewhere
elucidate
  elucidated

elucidating
elude
  He tried to elude
  his pursuers
eluded
eluding
elusive
elves *see* elf
emaciated
emanate
  emanated
  emanating
emanation
emancipate
  emancipated
  emancipating
emancipation
embalm
embankment
embargo
  pl embargoes
embark
embarkation
embarrass
  embarrassed
  embarrassing
embarrassment
embassy
  pl embassies
embellish
embellishment
ember
embezzle
  embezzled
  embezzling
embezzlement
emblazon
  emblazoned
  emblazoning

emblem
emblematic
embodiment
embody
  embodied
  embodying
emboss
embrace
  embraced
  embracing
embrocation
embroider
  embroidered
  embroidering
embroidery
embroil
  embroiled
  embroiling
embryo
  pl embryos
embryonic
emend
  to emend
  the manuscript
emendation
emerald
emerge
  emerged
  emerging
emergence
emergency
  pl emergencies
emergent
emery
emetic
emigrant
  an emigrant to America
  from Britain
emigrate

69

emigration
*emigration from
Britain*

eminence

eminent

eminently

emissary
pl emissaries

emission
the emission of gases

emit
emitted
emitting

emollient

emolument

emotion

emotional
adv emotionally

emotive

empathy

emperor

emphasis
*The emphasis must be
on hygiene: The
emphasis is on
the first syllable*

emphasize, -ise
*to emphasize its
value: to emphasized
the word 'new'*

emphasized
emphasizing

emphatic
adv emphatically

empire

empirical
adv empirically

empiricism

employ

employed
employing
employee
*He sacked
his young employee*

employer
*His employer
gave him a rise*

employment

empress
pl empresses

emptiness

empty
emptied
emptying

emu

emulate
emulated
emulating

emulation

emulsion

enable
enabled
enabling

enact

enamel
enamelled
enamelling

enamoured of

encampment

enchant

enchanter

enchantment

enchantress
pl enchantresses

enclose
enclosed
enclosing
enclosure

encompass

encore

encounter
encountered
encountering

encourage
encouraged
encouraging
encouragement

encroach

encroachment

encumbrance

encyclopaedia,
encyclopedia

encyclopaedic,
encyclopedic

end

endanger
endangered
endangering

endear
endeared
endearing
endearment

endeavour

endemic

ending

endive

endorse
endorsed
endorsing
endorsement

endow

endowment

endurance

endure
endured
enduring

enema

enemy
  pl enemies
energetic
  adv **energetically**
energy
  pl energies
enervate
  enervated
  enervating
enforce
  enforced
  enforcing
enforcement
engage
  engaged
  engaging
engagement
engine
engineer
  engineered
  engineering
engrave
  engraved
  engraving
engross
enhance
  enhanced
  enhancing
enigma
enigmatic
  adv enigmatically
enjoy
  enjoyed
  enjoying
enjoyable
enjoyment
enlarge
  enlarged
  enlarging

enlargement
enlighten
  enlightened
  enlightening
enlightenment
enlist
enliven
  enlivened
  enlivening
enmity
enormity
enormous
enough
enquire *see*
  inquire
enrage
  enraged
  enraging
enrol, enroll
  enrolled
  enrolling
enrolment
ensconce
  ensconced
  ensconcing
ensemble
ensign
ensue
  ensued
ensuing
ensure
  Great effort will
  ensure success
  ensured
  ensuring
entail
  entailed
  entailing
entangle

entangled
entangling
entanglement
enter
  entered
  entering
enterprise
enterprising
entertain
  entertained
  entertaining
entertainer
entertainment
enthral
  enthralled
  enthralling
enthuse
  enthused
  enthusing
enthusiasm
enthusiast
enthusiastic
  adv
  enthusiastically
entice
  enticed
  enticing
enticement
entire
entirely
entirety
entitle
  entitled
  entitling
entity
entomologist
  The entomologist
  studied the insects
entomology

entrails
'entrance
en'trance
  entranced
  entrancing
entrant
entreat
  entreated
  entreating
entreaty
  pl entreaties
entrenched
entrust
entry
  pl entries
enumerate
  enumerated
  enumerating
  enumeration
enunciate
  enunciated
  enunciating
  enunciation
envelop
  The mist began
  to envelop the hills
enveloped
  enveloping
envelope
  a brown envelope
enviable
  adv enviably
envious
environment
environmental
  adv environmen-
  tally
environmentalist
envisage

envisaged
envisaging
envoy
envy
  envied
  envying
enzyme
eon *see* aeon
epaulet, epaulette
ephemeral
  adv ephemerally
epic
epicure
epicurean
epidemic
epiglottis
epigram
  a witty epigram
epigrammatic
epilepsy
epileptic
epilogue
episcopacy
episcopal
episcopalian
episode
episodic
epistle
epitaph
  an epitaph
  on his grave
epithet
  'Great' was the
  epithet given to King
  Alfred
epitome
epitomize, -ise
  epitomized
  epitomizing

epoch
equable
  adv equably
equal
  adv equally
  equalled
  equalling
equality
equalize, -ise
  equalized
  equalizing
equanimity
equate
  equated
  equating
equation
equator
equatorial
equerry
  pl equerries
equestrian
equidistant
equilateral
equilibrium
equine
equinoctial
equinox
equip
  equipped
  equipping
equipment
equitable
  adv equitably
equity
equivalent
equivocal
  adv equivocally
equivocate
  equivocated

equivocating

era
  pl eras

eradicate
  eradicated
  eradicating

eradication

erase
  erased
  erasing

eraser

ere
  ere dawn

erect

erection

ermine

erode
  eroded
  eroding

erosion

erotic
  *erotic pictures
  of nudes*
  adv erotically

err
  to err is human
  erred
  erring

errand

errant

erratic
  an erratic driver
  adv erratically

erratum
  pl errata

erroneous

error

erudite
  adv eruditely

erudition

erupt

eruption

escalate
  escalated
  escalating

escalation

escalator

escapade

escape
  escaped
  escaping

escapement
  *the escapement
  of a watch*

escapism

escapist

escarpment
  a rocky escarpment

escort

escutcheon

Eskimo
  pl Eskimos

esoteric

esparto

especial
  adv especially

espionage

esplanade

Esq
  = Esquire
  John Brown Esq

essay
  *He wrote an essay
  on Shakespeare*

essayist

essence

essential
  adv essentially

establish

establishment

estate

esteem
  esteemed
  esteeming

estimate
  estimated
  estimating

estimation

estranged

estuary
  pl estuaries

etc
  = et cetera

etch

etching

eternal
  adv eternally

eternity

ether

ethereal
  adv ethereally

ethical
  adv ethically

ethics

ethnic

etiquette

etymological
  adv
  etymologically

etymologist
  *An etymologist
  is interested in words*

etymology
  pl etymologies

eucalyptus
  pl eucalypti,
  eucalyptuses

73

eulogize, -ise
  eulogized
  eulogizing
eulogy
  pl eulogies
euphemism
euphemistic
  adv
    euphemistically
euphonious
euphonium
euphoria
euphoric
  adv euphorically
eurhythmics
euthanasia
evacuate
  evacuated
  evacuating
evacuation
evacuee
evade
  evaded
  evading
evaluate
  evaluated
  evaluating
evaluation
evanescent
evangelical
evangelist
evaporate
  evaporated
  evaporating
evaporation
evasion
evasive
  adv evasively
eve

even
evening
evenness
event
eventful
  adv eventfully
eventual
  adv eventually
eventuality
  pl eventualities
ever
evergreen
evermore
every
everybody
everyone
everything
everywhere
evict
eviction
evidence
evident
evidently
evil
  adv evilly
evince
  evinced
  evincing
evocative
  adv evocatively
evoke
  evoked
  evoking
evolution
  the evolution of the
  species: Darwin's
  theory of evolution
evolutionary
evolve

evolved
evolving
ewe
  a ram and a ewe
ewer
exact
exacting
exactness
exaggerate
  exaggerated
  exaggerating
exaggeration
exalt
exaltation
exalted
examination
examine
  examined
  examining
examiner
example
exasperate
  exasperated
  exasperating
exasperation
excavate
  excavated
  excavating
excavation
excavator
exceed
exceedingly
excel
  excelled
  excelling
excellence
excellency
excellent
except

Nobody except John went: We enjoyed it except for the rain

excepting
exception
exceptional
 adv exceptionally
excerpt
excess
 an excess of alcohol
 pl excesses
excessive
 adv excessively
exchange
 exchanged
 exchanging
exchequer
ex'cise
 excised
 excising
'excise
excision
excitable
 adv excitably
excite
 excited
 exciting
excitement
exciting
exclaim
 exclaimed
 exclaiming
exclamation
exclamatory
exclude
 excluded
 excluding
exclusion
exclusive

adv exclusively
excommunicate
excommunication
excrement
excrescence
excrete
 excreted
 excreting
excruciating
excursion
excuse
 excused
 excusing
execrable
 adv execrably
execute
 executed
 executing
execution
executioner
 He was put to death by the executioner
executive
executor
 executor of his will
exemplary
exemplify
 exemplified
 exemplifying
exempt
exemption
exercise
 ballet exercises: exercises in spelling: to exercise your body

exercised
exercising
exert
exertion

exhaust
 exhausted
 exhausting
 exhaustion
 exhaustive
exhibit
 exhibited
 exhibiting
exhibition
exhibitionism
exhibitionist
exhibitor
exhilarate
 exhilarated
 exhilarating
exhort
exhortation
exhumation
exhume
 exhumed
 exhuming
exigency
 pl exigencies
exigent
exile
 exiled
 exiling
exist
existence
exit
 exited
 exiting
exodus
 pl exoduses
exonerate
 exonerated
 exoneration
exorbitance
exorbitant

exorcism
exorcist
exorcize, -ise
to exorcize the house of spirits
exorcized
exorcizing
exotic
adv **exotically**
expand
Metals expand when heated
expanse
expansion
expansive
a talkative and expansive person
expatiate
to expatiate about an experience
expatiated
expatiating
expatriate
expect
expected
expecting
expectancy
expectant
expectation
expedience
expediency
expedient
expedite
expedited
expediting
expedition
expeditious
expel
expelled

expelling
expend
to expend energy
expenditure
expense
expensive
expensive clothes
adv expensively
experience
experienced
experiencing
experiment
experimental
adv
    experimentally
expert
expertise
expiate
to expiate a crime
expiated
expiating
expire
expired
expiring
expiry
explain
explained
explaining
explanation
explanatory
expletive
explicable
adv explicably
explicit
explode
exploded
exploding
exploit
exploited

exploiting
exploitation
exploration
explore
explored
exploring
explorer
explosion
explosive
exponent
export
exportation
expose
exposed
exposing
exposition
exposure
expound
express
expression
expressive
adv expressively
expropriate
expropriated
expropriating
expropriation
expulsion
expurgate
expurgated
expurgating
exquisite
adv exquisitely
extant
Cannibalism is still extant in a few areas
extempore
extemporize, -ise
extemporized
extemporizing

extend
extension
extensive
 adv extensively
extent
extenuate
 extenuated
 extenuating
extenuation
exterior
exterminate
 exterminated
 exterminating
extermination
external
 adv externally
extinct
 The dodo is extinct:
 That volcano is now
 extinct

extinction
extinguish
extinguisher
extol
 extolled
 extolling
extort
extortion
extortionate
 adv extortionately
extra
extract
extraction
extradite
 extradited
 extraditing
extradition
extraneous
extraordinary

adv
 extraordinarily
extrasensory
extravagance
extravagant
extravert *see*
 extrovert
extreme
 adv extremely
extremist
extremity
 pl extremities
extricate
 extricated
 extricating
extrovert,
 extravert
exuberance
exuberant
exude
 exuded
 exuding
exult
exultant
exultation
eye
 eyed
 eying
eyebrow
eyelash
eyelid
eyrie, eyry, aerie
 an eagle's eyrie

F

fable
fabric
fabricate

fabricated
fabricating
fabrication
fabulous
façade
face
 faced
 facing
facet
facetious
facetiousness
facial
 adv facially
facile
 adv facilely
facilitate
 facilitated
 facilitating
facility
 pl facilities
facsimile
fact
faction
factious
factor
factory
 pl factories
factotum
faculty
 pl faculties
fad
faddy
fade
 faded
 fading
faeces
faerie, faery
 Spenser wrote the
 Faerie Queen: the

*magical land of
faerie*

fag

faggot

Fahrenheit

fail

  failed

  failing

failure

fain

  *Fain would he die
for love*

faint

  *She felt faint and
collapsed: a faint
noise: to faint in
the heat*

faintness

fair

  *Children enjoy a fair:
She has fair hair:
a fair attempt*

fairness

fairy

  *the fairy on the
Christmas tree: fairy
stories*

  pl fairies

faith

faithful

  adv faithfully

faithfulness

faithless

faithlessness

fake

  faked

  faking

falcon

falconry

fall

  fell

  He fell off the wall

  fallen

  *He has fallen off
the wall*

  falling

fallacious

fallacy

  pl fallacies

fallen *see* fall

fallibility

fallible

fallow

false

  adv falsely

falsehood

falseness

falsification

falsify

  falsified

  falsifying

falter

  faltered

  faltering

fame

familiar

familiarity

familiarize, -ise

  familiarized

  familiarizing

family

  pl families

famine

famished

famous

fan

  fanned

  fanning

fanatic

fanatical

  adv fanatically

fancier

fanciful

fancy

  pl fancies

  fancied

  fancying

fanfare

fang

fanlight

fantastic

  adv fantastically

fantasy

  pl fantasies

far

  compar farther

  superl farthest

farce

farcical

fare

  *bus fare:
How did you fare?*

  fared

  faring

farewell

farm

farmer

farrow

farther,

  farthest *see* far

farthing

fascinate

  fascinated

  fascinating

  fascination

fashion

  fashioned

fashioning
fashionable
   adv **fashionably**
fast
fasten
  fastened
  fastening
fastidious
fastness
fat
  compar **fatter**
  superl **fattest**
fatal
  adv **fatally**
fatality
  pl **fatalities**
fate
  a fate worse
  than death
fated
fateful
  adv **fatefully**
father
father-in-law
  pl **fathers-in-law**
fathom
  fathomed
  fathoming
fatigue
fatness
fatten
  fattened
  fattening
fatuous
fault
faultless
faulty
faun
  A faun is an

imaginary creature
fauna
favour
  favoured
  favouring
favourable
  adv **favourably**
favourite
favouritism
fawn
  fawn in colour:
  a deer and its fawn:
  Courtiers fawn
  on the king
fear
fearful
  adv **fearfully**
fearless
  adv **fearlessly**
feasibility
feasible
  adv **feasibly**
feast
feat
  a difficult feat
feather
feathery
feature
  featured
  featuring
February
fed *see* feed
federal
federated
federation
fee
feeble
  adv **feebly**
feebleness

feed
  fed
  feeding
feel
  felt
  feeling
feeler
feet *see* foot
feign
  Did she feign sleep?
  feigned
  feigning
feint
  a feint in fencing
felicitous
felicity
  pl **felicities**
feline
fell *see* fall
fell
  felled
  He felled the tree
  felling
fellow
fellowship
felon
felony
  pl **felonies**
felt *see* feel
felt
female
feminine
  adv **femininely**
femininity
feminism
feminist
femur
fen
fence

fenced
fencing
fend
fender
ferment

to ferment beer: in a ferment of excitement

fermentation
fern
ferocious
ferocity
ferret
  ferreted
  ferreting
ferrule
ferry
  pl ferries
  ferried
  ferrying
fertile
fertility
fertilization,
  -isation
fertilize, -ise
  fertilized
  fertilizing
fertilizer, -iser
fervent
fervour
fester
  festered
  festering
festival
festive
  adv festively
festivity
  pl festivities
festoon
  festooned

festooning
fetch
fête

a stall at the summer fête

fetid, foetid
fetish
  pl fetishes
fetlock
fetters
fettle
feud
feudal
feudalism
fever
fevered
feverish
few
fez
  pl fezzes
fiancé

He is her fiancé

fiancée

She is his fiancée

fiasco
  pl fiascos
fib
  fibbed
  fibbing
fibre
fibreglass
fibrous
fickle
fickleness
fiction
fictitious
fiddle
  fiddled
  fiddling

fidelity
fidget
  fidgeted
  fidgeting
field
field-marshal
fiend
fiendish
fierce
  adv fiercely
fierceness
fiery
fifteen
fifteenth
fifth
fiftieth
fifty
fig
fight
  fought
  fighting
fighter
figment
figurative
  adv figuratively
figure
  figured
figurehead
filament
filch
file
  filed

She filed the letter

  filing
filial
filigree
fill
  filled

We filled the bucket

filling
filler
fillet
fillip
filly
  pl fillies
film
filter
  filtered
  filtering
filth
filthy
fin
final
  a final separation
  adv finally
finale
  *the finale at the end
  of the concert*
finality
finalization,
  -isation
finalize, -ise
  finalized
  finalizing
finance
  financed
  financing
financial
  adv financially
financier
finch
  pl finches
find
  found
  He found the ball
  finding
fine
  fined

fining
finery
finesse
finger
  fingered
  fingering
fingerprint
finish
  finished
finite
Finnish
fiord, fjord
fir
  a fir tree: a fir cone
fire
  fired
  firing
fireworks
firm
firmament
firmness
first
first aid
firstly
firth
fiscal
fish
  pl fish
fisherman
fishmonger
fishy
fission
  nuclear fission
fissure
  a fissure in the rock
fist
fisticuffs
fit
  compar fitter

superl fittest
fitted
fitting
fitful
  adv fitfully
fitness
five
fix
fixedly
fixture
fizz
fizzle out
  fizzled out
  fizzling out
fizzy
fjord *see* fiord
flabbergasted
flabbiness
flabby
flaccid
flag
  flagged
  flagging
flagellation
flagon
flagrancy
flagrant
flail
  flailed
  flailing
flair
  *a flair for
  dressmaking*
flak
flake
  flaked
  flaking
flamboyance
flamboyant

flame
  flamed
  flaming
flamingo
  pl flamingos,
    flamingoes
flammable
  *Flammable material
  burns easily*
flan
flange
flank
flannel
flannelette
flap
  flapped
  flapping
flare
  *a flare as a signal:
  Did the fire flare up?*
  flared
  flaring
flash
  pl flashes
flashy
  adv flashily
flask
flat
  compar flatter
  superl flattest
flatness
flatten
  flattened
  flattening
flatter
  flattered
  flattering
flattery
flatulence

flatulent
flaunt
flavour
  flavoured
  flavouring
flaw
flawed
flawless
flax
flay
  flayed
  flaying
flea
  bitten by a flea
fleck
flecked
fled *see* flee
fledged
fledgling
flee
  to flee from the enemy
  fled
  fleeing
fleece
  fleeced
  fleecing
fleecy
fleet
fleeting
fleetness
flesh
fleshy
flew *see* fly
flex
flexibility
flexible
flick
flicker
  flickered

flickering
flight
flightiness
flighty
flimsy
flinch
fling
  flung
  flinging
flint
flip
  flipped
  flipping
flippancy
flippant
flipper
flirt
flirtation
flirtatious
flit
  flitted
  flitting
float
  floated
  floating
flock
  flocks of sheep
floe
  an ice floe
flog
  flogged
  flogging
flood
  flooded
  flooding
  floodlighting
floor
  floored
  flooring

flop
  flopped
  flopping
floppy
flora
floral
florid
florist
flotilla
flotsam
flounce
  flounced
  flouncing
flounder
  floundered
  floundering
flour
  Bread is made
  with flour
floury
  floury potatoes:
  My hands are floury
flourish
  pl flourishes
  flourished
  flourishing
flout
  flouted
  flouting
flow
  a flow of blood:
  to flow smoothly
  flowed
  flowing
flower
  a beautiful flower:
  Will that bush flower
  this year?
  flowered

flowering
flowery
  a flowery material:
  flowery language
flown *see* fly
fluctuate
  fluctuated
  fluctuating
fluctuation
flu
  a flu epidemic
flue
  The sweep cleaned
  the flue
fluency
fluent
fluff
fluffy
fluid
fluke
flung *see* fling
fluoridate
fluoridation
fluoride
fluoridize, -ise
  fluoridized
  fluoridizing
flurry
  pl flurries
  flurried
  flurrying
flush
  pl flushes
fluster
  flustered
  flustering
flute
  fluted
flutter

fluttered
fluttering
flux
fly
  pl flies
  flew
  The bird flew away:
  He flew the plane
  flown
  The bird has flown
  away: He has flown
  the plane
flyover
foal
  foaled
  foaling
foam
  foamed
  foaming
fob
fob off
  fobbed off
  fobbing off
fo'c'sle *see*
  forecastle
focus
  pl focuses, foci
  focused,
    focussed
  focusing,
    focussing
fodder
foe
foetid *see* fetid
fog
foggy
foil
  foiled
  foiling

told
folder
foliage
folk
folklore
folksong
follow
  followed
  following
follower
folly
  pl follies
foment
  to foment trouble
fond
fondle
  fondled
  fondling
fondness
font
  the baptismal font
food
fool
  fooled
  fooling
foolhardy
foolish
foolishness
foolproof
foolscap
foot
  pl feet
  These shoes hurt
  my feet
football
footing
footlights
footprint

footstep
footwear
for
forage
  foraged
  foraging
foray
forbade *see* forbid
forbear
  forbore
  forbearing
forbearance
forbearing
forbid
  forbade
  He forbade me to go
  forbidden
  He has forbidden me
  to go
  forbidding
forbore *see*
  forbear
force
  forced
  forcing
forceful
  adv forcefully
forceps
forcible
  adv forcibly
ford
fore
  well to the fore
forearm
foreboding
forecast
  forecast
  forecasting
forecastle, fo'c'sle

forefather
forefinger
forefront
foregone
  a foregone conclusion
foreground
forehead
foreign
foreigner
foreleg
forelock
foreman
  pl foremen
foremost
forensic
forerunner
foresee
  foresaw
  He foresaw the
  problem
  foreseen
  He has foreseen
  the problem
  foreseeing
foreshore
foresight
forest
forestall
  forestalled
  forestalling
forester
forestry
foretaste
foretell
  foretold
  foretelling
forethought
foretold *see*
  foretell

forewarn
forewoman
  pl forewomen
foreword
  *Who wrote the
  foreword
  to the book?*
forfeit
  forfeited
  forfeiting
forfeiture
forgave *see*
  forgive
forge
  forged
  forging
forgery
  pl forgeries
forget
  forgot
  He forgot it
  forgotten
  He has forgotten it
  forgetting
forgetful
  adv forgetfully
forgetfulness
forgive
  forgave
  He forgave her
  forgiven
  He has forgiven her
  forgiving
forgiveness
forgo
  forgoing
  forgone
  *He has forgone
  privileges*

forwent
  He forwent privileges
forgot, forgotten
  see forget
fork
forlorn
form
formal
  adv formally
formality
  pl formalities
format
formation
former
formerly
formidable
  adv formidably
formula
  pl formulae,
  formulas
formulate
  formulated
  formulating
formulation
forsake
  forsook
  She forsook religion
  forsaken
  *She has forsaken
  religion*
  forsaking
forswear
  forswore
  He forswore alcohol
  forsworn
  *He has forsworn
  alcohol*
  forswearing
fort

They besieged the fort
forte
  Singing is his forte
forth
  *issuing forth:
  giving forth*
forthcoming
forthright
forthwith
fortieth
fortification
fortify
  fortified
  fortifying
fortitude
fortnight
fortnightly
fortress
  pl fortresses
fortuitous
fortunate
  adv **fortunately**
fortune
forty
  He spent forty pounds
forum
  pl forums
forward
  forward not backward
forwards
forwent *see* forgo
fossil
foster
  fostered
  fostering
fought *see* fight
foul
  *the foul smell of
  tobacco: foul weather*

found *see* find
found
  founded
    He founded the business
  founding
  foundation
  founder
  foundered
  foundering
  foundling
  foundry
    pl foundries
  fount
    the fount of knowledge
  fountain
  four
    Four and four makes eight
  fourteen
  fourteenth
  fourth
    He was fourth in the race
  fowl
    fish and fowl
  fox
    pl foxes
  foxglove
  foxtrot
  foxy
  foyer
  fracas
    pl fracas
  fraction
  fractional
    adv fractionally
  fractious
  fracture

fractured
fracturing
fragile
fragment
fragmentary
fragrance
fragrant
frail
frailty
  pl frailties
frame
  framed
  framing
framework
franc
  the French franc
franchise
frank
  a frank statement: frank and honest
frank
  to frank a letter
frankfurter
frankincense
frantic
  adv frantically
fraternal
fraternity
fraternization, -isation
fraternize, -ise
  fraternized
  fraternizing
fraud
fraudulent
fraught
fray
  frayed
  fraying

freak
freakish
freckle
free
freedom
freelance
freely
freeze
  to freeze vegetables
  froze
    She froze the meat
  frozen
    She has frozen the peas
  freezing
freight
freighter
French
frenetic
  adv frenetically
frenzied
frenzy
frequency
  pl frequencies
frequent
fresco
  pl frescoes, frescos
fresh
freshen
  freshened
  freshening
fret
  fretted
  fretting
fretful
  adv fretfully
fretwork
friar

friary
  pl friaries
friction
Friday
fridge
fried *see* fry
friend
friendliness
friendly
friendship
frieze
  a ceiling frieze
frigate
fright
frighten
  frightened
  frightening
frightful
  adv frightfully
frigid
frigidity
frill
frilly
fringe
  fringed
  fringing
Frisbee®
frisk
frisky
  adv friskily
fritter
  frittered
  frittering
frivolity
  pl frivolities
frivolous
frizzy
fro
frock

frog
frogman
  pl frogmen
frolic
  frolicked
  frolicking
frolicsome
from
frond
front
frontage
frontier
frontispiece
frost
frosted
frosty
  adv frostily
froth
frothy
frown
froze, frozen *see*
  freeze
frugal
  adv frugally
frugality
fruit
fruiterer
fruitful
  adv fruitfully
fruition
fruitless
  adv fruitlessly
frump
frumpish
frustrate
  frustrated
  frustrating
frustration
fry

fried
frying
fuchsia
fuddle
  fuddled
  fuddling
fudge
fuel
fugitive
fugue
fulcrum
  pl fulcrums,
  fulcra
fulfil
  fulfilled
  fulfilling
fulfilment
full
fullness
fully
fulmar
fulminate
  fulminated
  fulminating
fulsome
  adv fulsomely
fumble
  fumbled
  fumbling
fume
  fumed
  fuming
  fumes
fumigate
  fumigated
  fumigating
fumigation
fun
function

functioned
functioning
functional
  adv functionally
fund
fundamental
  adv
    fundamentally
funeral
  He attended her
  funeral
funereal
  solemn, funereal music
funfair
fungus
  pl fungi,
    funguses
funicular railway
funnel
funny
  adv funnily
fur
  a fur coat:
  a cat's fur
furbish
furious
furlong
furnace
furnish
furnishings
furniture
furore
furrier
furrow
furry
further
  furthered
  furthering
furthermore
88

furthest
furtive
  adv furtively
fury
fuse
fused
fusing
fuselage
fusion
fuss
fussed
fussing
fussy
  adv fussily
fusty
futile
  adv futilely
futility
future
fuzz
fuzzy

G

gabble
  the noisy gabble of
  the crowd: to gabble
  noisily
gabbled
gabbling
gaberdine
gable
  the gable of a house
gadget
Gaelic
gaff
  a fishing gaff:
  blow the gaff
gaffe

  a social gaffe
gag
gagged
gagging
gaggle
gaiety
gaily *see* gay
gain
gained
gaining
gait
  a shuffling gait
gaiter
gala
galaxy
  pl galaxies
gale
gall
gallant
gallantry
gallbladder
galleon
  a Spanish galleon
gallery
  pl galleries
galley
  pl galleys
galling
gallon
  a gallon of petrol
gallop
  galloped
  galloping
gallows
galore
galoshes
galvanize, -ise
  galvanized
  galvanizing

galvanometer
gambit
gamble
  to gamble on a horse
  gambled
  gambling
gambol
  The lambs gambol
  gambolled
  gambolling
game
gamekeeper
gaming
gammon
gamut
gander
gang
ganger
gangrene
gangrenous
gangster
gang up
  ganged up
  ganging up
gangway
gannet
gantry
  pl gantries
gaol *see* jail
gaoler *see* jailer
gap
gape
  gaped
  gaping
garage
  garaged
  garaging
garb
garbage

garbed
garbled
garden
  gardened
  gardening
gardener
gargantuan
gargle
  gargled
  gargling
gargoyle
garish
garland
garlic
garment
garnet
garnish
  pl garnishes
garret
garrison
  garrisoned
  garrisoning
garrotte
  garrotted
  garrotting
garrulity
garrulous
garter
gas
  pl gases
  gassed
  gassing
gaseous
gash
  pl gashes
gasometer
gasp
gastric
gate

  a garden gate
gâteau
  pl gâteaux
gatecrash
gatecrasher
gather
  gathered
  gathering
gathering
gauche
gaucho
  pl gauchos
gaudiness
gaudy
  adv gaudily
gauge
  gauged
  gauging
gaunt
gauntlet
gauze
gave *see* give
gavotte
gawky
  adv gawkily
gay
  adv gaily
gaze
  gazed
  gazing
gazelle
gazette
  gazetted
  gazetting
gazetteer
gear
gear to
  geared to
  gearing to

geese *see* goose
geisha
gelatine
gelatinous
gelding
gem
gender
gene
genealogical
genealogist
genealogy
  pl genealogies
genera *see* genus
general
  adv generally
generalization,
  -isation
generalize, -ise
  generalized
  generalizing
generate
  generated
  generating
generation
generator
generosity
generous
genesis
genetic
  adv genetically
genetics
genial
  adv genially
genie
  a magic genie
genius
  *He is clever but
  not a genius*
  pl geniuses
90

genteel
  a genteel tea-party
  adv genteelly
gentile
  *He is a gentile,
  not a Jew*
gentility
gentle
  *She has a kind, gentle
  nature: a gentle
  breeze*
  adv gently
gentleman
  pl gentlemen
gentlemanly
gentleness
gentry
genuine
  adv genuinely
genuineness
genus
  *To what genus does
  that plant belong?*
  pl genera
geographical
  adv geographi-
  cally
geography
geological
  adv geologically
geologist
geology
geometric
  adv geometrically
geometry
geranium
gerbil
germ
German

germane
germinate
  germinated
  germinating
germination
gesticulate
  gesticulated
  gesticulating
gesticulation
gesture
  gestured
  gesturing
get
  got
  getting
geyser
ghastliness
ghastly
gherkin
ghetto
  pl ghettos
ghost
ghostliness
ghostly
ghoul
ghoulish
giant
giantess
gibber
  gibbered
  gibbering
gibberish
gibbet
gibbon
gibe *see* jibe
giblets
giddiness
giddy
gift

gifted
gigantic
giggle
  giggled
  giggling
gild
  to gild a brooch:
  to gild the lily
gill
gillie
gilt
  a brooch covered
  in gilt
gimcrack
gimlet
gimmick
gin
ginger
gingerly
gingham
gipsy *see* gypsy
giraffe
gird
girder
girdle
girl
girlhood
girlish
giro
girth
gist
give
  gave
  He gave her a present
  given
  He has given her
  a present
  giving
glacé

glacier
  The glacier is melting
glad
gladden
  gladdened
  gladdening
glade
gladiator
gladness
glamorous
glamour
glance
  glanced
  glancing
gland
glandular
glare
  glared
  glaring
glass
  pl glasses
glassy
  adv glassily
glaze
  glazed
  glazing
glazier
  The glazier mended
  the window
gleam
  gleamed
  gleaming
glean
  gleaned
  gleaning
glee
gleeful
  adv gleefully
glen

glib
glibness
glide
  glided
  gliding
glider
glimmer
  glimmered
  glimmering
glimpse
  glimpsed
  glimpsing
glint
glisten
  glistened
  glistening
glitter
  glittered
  glittering
gloaming
gloat
global
  adv globally
globe
globular
globule
gloom
gloomy
  adv gloomily
glorify
  glorified
  glorifying
glorious
glory
  pl glories
gloss
  pl glosses
glossary
  pl glossaries

glossy
  adv glossily
glove
glow
  glowed
  glowing
glower
  glowered
  glowering
glucose
glue
  glued
  gluing
gluey
glum
glut
  glutted
  glutting
glutton
gluttonous
gluttony
glycerine
gnarled
gnash
gnat
gnaw
gnome
gnu
go
  went
  He went yesterday
  gone
  He has gone away
  going
goad
go-ahead
goal
  He scored a goal
goat

gobble
  gobbled
  gobbling
goblet
goblin
god
goddess
  pl goddesses
godfather
godliness
godly
godmother
goggles
going *see* go
goitre
gold
golden
goldfish
golf
  golfed
  golfing
golfer
golliwog,
  gollywog
gondola
gondolier
gone *see* go
gong
good
  compar better
  superl best
  adv well
goodbye
good-day
goodly
goodness
goodwill
goose
  pl geese

gooseberry
  pl gooseberries
goose-pimples
gore
  gored
  goring
gorge
  gorged
  gorging
gorgeous
gorgon
gorgonzola
gorilla
  A gorilla is an ape
gorse
gory
gosling
gospel
gossamer
gossip
  gossiped
  gossiping
got *see* get
gouache
gouge
  gouged
  gouging
goulash
  pl goulashes
gourd
gourmand
  *He is a greedy
  gourmand*
gourmet
  *He likes good food and
  wine – he is a gourmet*
gout
govern
  governed

governing
governess
  pl governesses
government
governor
gown
grab
  grabbed
  grabbing
grace
  graced
  gracing
graceful
  adv gracefully
gracefulness
gracious
graciousness
gradation
  gradation in order
  of difficulty
grade
  graded
  grading
gradient
gradual
  adv gradually
gradualness
graduate
  graduated
  graduating
graduation
  graduation from
  University
graffiti
graft
Grail
grain
gram *see* gramme
grammar

grammatical
  adv
  grammatically
gramme, gram
gramophone
granary
  pl granaries
grand
grandchild
  pl grandchildren
grand-daughter
grandeur
grandfather
grandiloquent
grandiose
grandmother
grandson
grandstand
granite
granny
  pl grannies
grant
granular
granule
grape
grapefruit
graph
graphic
graphite
grapple
  grappled
  grappling
grasp
grass
  pl grasses
grasshopper
grassy
grate
  a fire in the grate

grateful
  adv gratefully
grater
gratification
gratify
  gratified
  gratifying
grating
gratis
gratitude
gratuitous
gratuity
  pl gratuities
grave
  adv gravely
gravel
graven
graveyard
gravitate
  gravitated
  gravitating
gravitation
gravity
gravy
gray *see* grey
graze
  grazed
  grazing
grease
  greased
  greasing
greasy
great
  a great man;
  a great amount
greatness
greed
greediness
greedy

adv greedily
green
greenery
greenfly
greengage
greengrocer
greenhouse
greenish
greenness
greet
  greeted
  greeting
greetings
gregarious
grenade
grew *see* grow
grey, gray
greyhound
grid
griddle
grief
  full of grief
  at his death
grievance
grieve
  to grieve over
  his death
  grieved
  grieving
grievous
griffin, griffon
grill
  a grill on a cooker:
  a mixed grill:
  to grill a steak
grille
  a metal grille
  in a window
grim

grimace
  grimaced
  grimacing
grime
grimness
grin
  grinned
  grinning
grind
  ground
  He ground the coffee
  grinding
grinder
grindstone
grip
  gripped
  He gripped her hand
  gripping
gripe
  griped
  He griped about
  the service
  griping
gripped *see* grip
grisly
  a grisly, horrible
  sight
grist
gristle
gristly
  gristly meat
grit
  gritted
  gritting
grizzled
grizzly
  a grizzly bear
groan
  groaned

groaning
groat
grocer
grocery
  pl groceries
groggy
  adv groggily
groin
groom
  groomed
  grooming
groove
groovy
grope
  to grope one's way:
  to grope for a
  handkerchief
  groped
  groping
gross
  grossly
  grossness
grotesque
  adv grotesquely
  grotesqueness
grotto
  pl grottos,
    grottoes
ground *see* grind
ground
  grounded
  They grounded
  the planes
  grounding
  grounding
  groundless
  groundsel
  groundwork
group

94

a group of children:
to group together
grouped
grouping
grouse
to shoot a grouse
pl grouse
grouse
a grouse about prices
pl grouses
groused
grousing
grove
grovel
grovelled
grovelling
grow
grew
He grew tall
grown
He has grown tall
growing
growl
grown *see* grow
growth
grub
grubbed
grubbing
grubbiness
grubby
adv grubbily
grudge
grudged
grudging
gruel
gruelling
gruesome
gruff
grumble

grumbled
grumbling
grumpy
adv grumpily
grunt
guarantee
guaranteed
guaranteeing
guarantor
guard
guardian
guava
guerrilla
guerrilla warfare
guess
pl guesses
guessed
guessing
guest
guffaw
guidance
guide
guided
guiding
guidebook
guild
a guild of craftsmen
guile
guileless
guillemot
guillotine
guillotined
guillotining
guilt
the guilt of
the prisoner
guilty
adv guiltily
guinea

guinea-fowl
guinea-pig
guise
guitar
gulf
pl gulfs
gull
gullet
gullible
adv gullibly
gully
pl gullies
gulp
gum
gummed
gumming
gummy
gumption
gun
gunned
gunning
gunfire
gunpowder
gunwale, gunnel
gurgle
gurgled
gurgling
gush
gusset
gust
gusto
gusty
adv gustily
gut
gutted
gutting
guts
gutter
guttersnipe

guttural
  adv gutturally
guy
  pl guys
gym
gymkhana
gymnasium
  pl gymnasiums,
    gymnasia
gymnast
gymnastics
gypsy, gipsy
  pl gypsies,
    gipsies
gyrate
  gyrated
  gyrating
  gyratory

H

haberdasher
haberdashery
habit
habitable
habitat
habitation
habitual
  adv habitually
habituate
  habituated
  habituating
hack
hackles
hackney
hackneyed
hacksaw
haddock
Hades

haemoglobin
haemorrhage
  haemorrhaged
  haemorrhaging
hag
haggard
haggis
  pl haggises
haggle
  haggled
  haggling
ha-ha
hail
  hail and wind:
  to hail a taxi
  hailed
  hailing
hailstone
hair
  a hair of her head
hairdresser
hair-raising
hairy
hake
halberd
halcyon
hale
  hale and hearty
half
  half an apple
  pl halves
halfpenny
  pl halfpennies
halibut
halitosis
hall
hallmark
hallo *see* hello
hallow

  to hallow a shrine
Hallowe'en
hallucinate
  hallucinated
  hallucinating
hallucination
halo
  a saint's halo
  pl halos, haloes
halt
halter
halting
halve
  to halve an apple
  halved
  halving
halves *see* half
ham
hamburger
hamfisted
hamlet
hammer
hammered
  hammering
hammock
hamper
  hampered
  hampering
hamster
hamstring
  hamstrung
  hamstringing
hand
handbag
handcuffs
handful
  pl **handfuls**
handicap
handicapped

handicraft
handiness
handiwork
handkerchief
   pl handkerchiefs,
   handkerchieves
handle
   handled
   handling
handlebars
handsome
   adv handsomely
handsomeness
handwriting
handy
handyman
hang
   hung
   A picture hung on the wall: He hung his coat up

   hanged
   They hanged the murderer

   hanging
hangar
   a hangar for two planes

hanger
   a coat hanger
hanger-on
   pl hangers-on
hangover
hank
hanker
   hankered
   hankering
hankie, hanky
   pl hankies

hansom-cab
haphazard
hapless
happen
   happened
   happening
happiness
happy
   compar happier
   superl happiest
   adv happily
happy-go-lucky
hara-kiri
harangue
   harangued
   haranguing
harass
   harassed
   harassing
   harassment
harbinger
harbour
   harboured
   harbouring
hard
harden
   hardened
   hardening
hardiness
hardly
hardness
hardware
hardy
   adv hardily
hare
   a hare and a rabbit
harebell
hare-brained
hare-lip

harem
hark
hark back
   harked back
   harking back
harlequin
harm
harmful
   adv harmfully
harmless
harmonica
harmonious
harmonium
harmonize, -ise
   harmonized
   harmonizing
harmony
harness
   pl harnesses
harp
harpist
harp on
harpoon
harpsichord
harpy
   pl harpies
harrier
harrow
harrowing
harry
   harried
   harrying
harsh
harshness
hart
   a hart and a hind
harvest
harvester
hash

hassock
haste
hasten
  hastened
  hastening
hasty
  adv hastily
hat
hatch
  pl hatches
hatchery
  pl hatcheries
hatchet
hatchway
hate
  hated
  hating
hateful
  adv hatefully
hatred
hatter
haughtiness
haughty
  adv haughtily
haul
  hauled
  hauling
haulage
haunch
  pl haunches
haunt
have
  had
  having
haven
haversack
havoc
haw
hawk

hawker
hawthorn
hay
hay-fever
haystack
haywire
hazard
hazardous
haze
hazel
haziness
hazy
  adv hazily
he
head
  headed
  heading
headache
head-dress
header
heading
headlight
headline
headmaster
headmistress
  pl
    headmistresses
headquarters
headstrong
headway
heady
heal
  to heal a wound
  healed
  healing
health
healthy
  adv healthily
heap

heaped
heaping
hear
  She cannot hear you
  heard
  hearing
hearsay
hearse
heart
  heart disease:
  a loving heart
heartburn
hearten
  heartened
  heartening
heartfelt
hearth
heartless
hearty
  adv heartily
heat
  heated
  heating
heath
heathen
heather
heave
  heaved
  heaving
heaven
heavenly
heave to
  hove to
  heaving to
heaviness
heavy
  compar heavier
  superl heaviest
  adv heavily

heckle
  heckled
  heckling
heckler
hectare
hectic
  adv hectically
hector
  hectored
  hectoring
he'd
  = he had, he
  would
hedge
  hedged
  hedging
hedgehog
hedgerow
heed
heedless
heel
  the heel of a shoe:
  to heel a shoe
  heeled
  heeling
hefty
heifer
height
heighten
  heightened
  heightening
heinous
heinousness
heir
  heir to the throne:
  heir to a fortune
heiress
  pl heiresses
heirloom

held *see* hold
helicopter
heliotrope
helium
he'll
  = he will
hell
hellish
hello, hallo, hullo
  Hello there!:
  Hallo! How are you?
helm
helmet
helmsman
help
helpful
  adv helpfully
helpfulness
helping
helpless
helplessness
helter-skelter
hem
  hemmed
  hemming
hemisphere
hemispherical
hemlock
hemp
hen
hence
henceforth
henchman
henna
henpecked
heptagon
heptagonal
her
herald

heraldic
heraldry
herb
herbaceous
herbal
herbalist
herbivore
herbivorous
Herculean
herd
here
  Here you are:
  I left it here
hereabouts
hereafter
hereby
hereditary
heredity
heresy
  pl heresies
heretic
heretical
  adv heretically
heritage
hermaphrodite
hermetically
hermit
hermitage
hero
  pl heroes
heroic
  adv heroically
heroine
heroism
heron
  a heron eating fish
herring
  fried herring
hers

herself
hertz
he's
  = he is, he has
hesitancy
hesitant
hesitate
  hesitated
  hesitating
hesitation
hessian
het up
hew
  to hew down a tree
  hewed
  He hewed down a tree
  hewed, hewn
  He has hewed down a tree: He has hewn it down

  hewing
hexagon
hexagonal
heyday
hibernate
  hibernated
  hibernating
hibernation
hiccup, hiccough
hide
  hid
  He hid the treasure
  hidden
  He has hidden the treasure
hidebound
hideous
hiding
hierarchy

hieroglyphics
hi-fi
higgledy-piggledy
high
  compar higher
  at a higher level
  superl highest
highbrow
high fidelity
Highlands
highlight
highly
highness
highway
hijack
  hijacked
  hijacking
  hijacker
hike
  hiked
  hiking
  hiker
hilarious
hilarity
hill
hillock
hilly
hilt
him
  She killed him
himself
hind
hinder
  hindered
  hindering
hindmost
hindrance
hindsight
hinge

hinged
hinging
hint
hinterland
hip
hippopotamus
  pl hippopota-
    muses,
    hippopotami
hire
  to hire a car
  hired
  hiring
hire purchase
hirsute
his
hiss
  pl hisses
historian
historic
historical
  adv historically
history
  pl histories
histrionics
hit
  hit
  hitting
hitch
  pl hitches
hitchhike
  hitchhiked
  hitchhiking
hither
hitherto
hive
hoar
  hoar frost
hoard

to hoard food
hoarding
hoarse
*She is hoarse
from shouting*
adv **hoarsely**
hoary
hoax
pl **hoaxes**
hob
hobble
 hobbled
 hobbling
hobby
 pl **hobbies**
hobby-horse
hobgoblin
hobnail
hobnob
 hobnobbed
 hobnobbing
hock
hockey
hocus-pocus
hod
hoe
 hoed
 hoeing
hog
 hogged
 hogging
Hogmanay
hoist
hold
 held
 holding
holdall
holder
holding

hold-up
hole
 *a hole in the ground:
 a hole in her sock*
holiday
holiness
hollow
holly
hollyhock
holocaust
holster
holt
holy
homage
home
 homed
 homing
homeliness
homely
home-made
homesick
homestead
homewards
homework
homicidal
homicide
homing
**homogenization,
 -isation**
homogenize, -ise
 homogenized
 homogenizing
homonym
hone
 honed
 honing
honest
honesty
honey

honeycomb
honeyed
honeymoon
honeysuckle
honk
honorarium
honorary
*He is honorary
secretary of the club*
honour
honoured
honouring
honourable
*He is an honest and
honourable man*
adv **honourably**
hood
hoodwink
hoof
 pl **hooves, hoofs**
hook
hookah, hooka
hooked
hooligan
hooliganism
hoop
 a hoop round a barrel
hooray
hoot
 hooted
 hooting
hooter
Hoover ®
hoover
 hoovered
 hoovering
hop
 hopped
 The bird hopped over

hopping
hope
  hoped
  She hoped that he
  would come
  hoping
hopeful
hopefully
hopefulness
hopeless
hopelessness
hopped *see* hop
hopper
hopscotch
horde
  a horde of
  noisy children
horizon
horizontal
horn
hornet
hornpipe
horny
horoscope
horrendous
horrible
  adv horribly
horrid
horrify
  horrified
  horrifying
horror
horse
  two dogs and a horse
horseplay
horsepower
horseshoe
horticultural
horticulture

horticulturist
hosanna
hose
hosiery
hospitable
  adv hospitably
hospital
hospitality
host
hostage
hostel
hostelry
  pl hostelries
hostess
  pl hostesses
hostile
  adv hostilely
hostility
  pl hostilities
hot
  compar hotter
  superl hottest
hotchpotch
hot-dog
hotel
hotfoot
hot-headed
hothouse
hound
hour
hourly
house
  housed
  housing
household
householder
housekeeper
housewife
hovel

hover
  hovered
  hovering
hovercraft
hove to *see* heave
  to
how
howdah
however
howl
howler
hub
hubbub
huddle
  huddled
  huddling
hue
  the hue of the sky:
  a hue and cry
huff
huffy
hug
  hugged
  hugging
huge
  adv hugely
hugeness
hula-hoop
hulk
hulking
hull
hullabaloo
hullo *see* hello
hum
  hummed
  humming
human
  a human being
humane

cruel, not humane
adv humanely
humanism
humanist
humanitarian
humanity
humble
  adv humbly
humdrum
humid
humidity
humiliate
  humiliated
  humiliating
humiliation
  full of shame
  and humiliation
humility
  meekness and humility
humorist
humorous
humour
hump
humpbacked
humus
hunch
  pl hunches
hundred
hundredth
hundredweight
hung *see* hang
hunger
  hungered
  hungering
hungry
  adv hungrily
hunt
hunter
huntress

pl huntresses
huntsman
  pl huntsmen
hurdle
  hurdled
  hurdling
hurdygurdy
hurl
hurlyburly
hurrah
hurray
hurricane
hurry
  hurried
  hurrying
hurt
hurtful
  adv hurtfully
hurtle
  hurtled
  hurtling
husband
husbandry
hush
hush-hush
husk
husky
  pl huskies
hussar
hussy
  pl hussies
hustings
hustle
  hustled
  hustling
hut
hutch
  pl hutches
hyacinth

hyaena *see* hyena
hybrid
hydra
hydrant
hydraulic
hydro
hydroelectric
hydrogen
hydropathic
hydrophobia
hyena, hyaena
hygiene
hygienic
  adv hygienically
hymn
  The choir sang a hymn
hymnal
hymnary
  pl hymnaries
hyperactive
hyperbole
hypermarket
hyphen
hypnosis
hypnotic
  adv hypnotically
hypnotism
hypnotist
hypnotize, -ise
  hypnotized
  hypnotizing
hypochondria
hypochondriac
hypocrisy
hypocrite
hypocritical
  adv hypocritically
hypodermic
hypotenuse

hypothesis
  pl hypotheses
hypothetical
  adv
    hypothetically
hysteria
hysterical
  adv hysterically
hysterics

I

ice
  iced
  icing
iceberg
icecream
icicle
icing
icon, ikon
iconoclasm
icy
  adv icily
I'd
  = I had, I should,
    I would
idea
ideal
  adv ideally
idealism
idealist
idealize, -ise
  idealized
  idealizing
identical
  adv identically
identification
identify
  identified

identifying
identikit (picture)
identity
  pl identities
ideological
  adv ideologically
ideology
idiocy
  pl idiocies
idiom
idiomatic
  adv idiomatically
idiosyncrasy
  pl idiosyncrasies
idiosyncratic
  adv idiosyncrati-
    cally
idiot
idiotic
  adv idiotically
idle
  a slow and idle worker
  adv idly
  to idle away time
  idled
  idling
idleness
idly *see* idle
idol
  The pop-star is her
  idol: heathen idols
idolize, -ise
  idolized
  idolizing
idyll
idyllic
  adv idyllically
if
igloo

pl igloos
igneous
ignite
  ignited
  igniting
ignition
ignoble
  adv ignobly
ignominious
ignominy
ignoramus
  pl ignoramuses
ignorance
ignorant
ignore
  ignored
  ignoring
iguana
ikon *see* icon
I'll
  = I shall, I will
ill
  compar **worse**
  superl **worst**
illegal
  adv illegally
illegibility
illegible
  untidy and illegible
  handwriting
  adv illegibly
illegitimacy
illegitimate
  adv illegitimately
illicit
  an illicit love affair
illiteracy
illiterate
  He cannot read that

letter — he is illiterate

illness
  pl illnesses
illogical
  adv illogically
illuminate
  illuminated
  illuminating
illumination
illusion
  an optical illusion:
  an illusion of
  grandeur

illustrate
  illustrated
  illustrating
illustration
illustrative
illustrator
illustrious
I'm
  = I am
image
imagery
imaginary
imagination
imaginative
  adv imaginatively
imagine
  imagined
  imagining
imbecile
imbibe
  imbibed
  imbibing
imbue
  imbued
  imbuing
imitate

imitated
imitating
imitation
immaculate
  adv immaculately
immaterial
immature
immediacy
immediate
  adv immediately
immemorial
immense
  adv immensely
immensity
immerse
  immersed
  immersing
immersion
immigrant
  immigrants to Britain
immigration
  immigration into Britain
imminent
immobile
immobility
immobilize, -ise
  immobilized
  immobilizing
immoderate
immoral
  wicked and immoral
immorality
  wickedness and
  immorality
immortal
  People die —
  they are not immortal
immortality
  the immortality of God

immortalize, -ise
  immortalized
  immortalizing
immovable
  adv immovably
immune
immunity
immunize, -ise
  immunized
  immunizing
imp
impact
impair
  impaired
  impairing
impairment
impale
  impaled
  impaling
impart
impartial
  adv impartially
impartiality
impassable
impasse
impassioned
impassive
  adv impassively
impatience
impatient
impeach
impeccable
  adv impeccably
impecunious
impede
  impeded
  impeding
impediment
impel

impelled
impelling
impending
imperative
  adv imperatively
imperceptible
  adv imperceptibly
imperfect
imperfection
imperial
imperialism
imperil
  imperilled
  imperilling
imperious
impermeable
impersonal
  adv impersonally
impersonate
  impersonated
  impersonating
impersonation
impersonator
impertinence
impertinent
imperturbable
impervious
impetigo
impetuosity
impetuous
  rash and impetuous
impetus
  the impetus of
  the blow
impiety
impinge
  impinged
  impinging
impious

impish
implement
implicate
  implicated
  implicating
implication
implicit
imply
  implied
  implying
impolite
  adv impolitely
import
importance
important
importation
importunate
importune
  importuned
  importuning
importunity
impose
  imposed
  imposing
imposition
impossibility
impossible
  adv impossibly
impostor
impotence
impotent
impound
impoverish
impracticability
impracticable
  an impracticable idea
  adv impracticably
impractical
  an impractical person

  adv impractically
impracticality
impregnable
impregnate
impresario
  pl impresarios
impress
impression
impressionable
impressionism
impressive
  adv impressively
imprint
imprison
  imprisoned
  imprisoning
  imprisonment
improbability
improbable
  adv improbably
impromptu
improper
impropriety
  pl improprieties
improve
  improved
  improving
improvement
improvidence
improvident
improvisation
improvise
  improvised
  improvising
impudence
impudent
impulse
impulsive
  adv impulsively

impulsiveness
impunity
impure
impurity
  pl impurities
imputation
impute
  imputed
  imputing
in
  in the house:
  dressed in black:
  covered in dirt

inability
inaccessible
  adv inaccessibly
inaccurate
  adv inaccurately
inaction
inactive
inactivity
inadequacy
  pl inadequacies
inadequate
  adv inadequately
inadmissible
inadvertent
inane
  adv inanely
inanimate
inanity
  pl inanities
inapplicable
inappropriate
  adv
    inappropriately
inapt
  an inapt remark
inarticulate

inasmuch as
inattention
inattentive
  adv inattentively
inaudible
  adv inaudibly
inaugural
inaugurate
  inaugurated
  inaugurating
inauguration
inauspicious
inborn
inbred
inbreeding
incalculable
incandescent
incantation
incapable
incapacitate
  incapacitated
  incapacitating
incapacity
incarcerate
  incarcerated
  incarcerating
incarnate
incarnation
incendiary
in'cense
  incensed
  incensing
'incense
incentive
inception
incessant
inch
  pl inches
incidence

incident
incidental
  adv incidentally
incinerator
incipient
incision
incisive
  adv incisively
incisiveness
incisor
incite
  incited
  inciting
incitement
incivility
  pl incivilities
inclemency
inclement
inclination
incline
  inclined
  inclining
include
  included
  including
inclusion
inclusive
  adv inclusively
incognito
incoherence
incoherent
incombustible
income
incoming
incommode
  incommoded
  incommoding
incommunicado
incomparable

adv
  incomparably
incompatibility
incompatible
incompetence
incompetent
incomprehensible
adv
  incomprehens-
    ibly
incomprehension
inconceivable
adv inconceiv-
  ably
inconclusive
adv inconclus-
  ively
incongruity
incongruous
adv
  incongruously
inconsequential
adv inconsequen-
  tially
inconsiderable
inconsiderate
adv
  inconsiderately
inconsistent
inconspicuous
inconstancy
inconstant
incontinence
incontinent
inconvenience
inconvenient
incontrovertible
adv
  incontrovertibly

incorporate
incorporated
incorporating
incorrect
incorrigible
adv incorrigibly
incorruptible
increase
increased
increasing
increasingly
incredibility
incredible
  an incredible story
adv incredibly
incredulity
incredulous
  an incredulous person:
  an incredulous look
increment
incriminate
incriminated
incriminating
incubate
incubated
incubating
incubation
incubator
inculcate
inculcated
inculcating
incumbent
incur
incurred
incurring
incurable
adv incurably
incursion
indebted

indebtedness
indecency
indecent
indecision
indecisive
adv indecisively
indeed
indefatigable
adv indefatigably
indefensible
adv indefensibly
indefinable
adv indefinably
indefinite
adv indefinitely
indelible
adv indelibly
indelicacy
indelicate
adv indelicately
indemnity
indent
indentation
indenture
independence
independent
indescribable
adv indescribably
indestructible
indeterminate
adv
  indeterminately
index
  pl indexes,
    indices
  indexes of books:
  indices of numbers
Indian
indicate

indicated
indicating
indication
indicative
indicator
indices *see* index
indict [in'dīt]
indictment
indifference
indifferent
indigence
indigenous

*Tobacco is not
indigenous to Britain*

indigent

the indigent widow

indigestible
indigestion
indignant
indignation
indignity

pl indignities

indigo
indirect
indiscreet
indiscretion
indiscriminate

adv indiscrimin-
ately

indispensable

adv indispensably

indisposed
indisposition
indisputable

adv indisputably

indistinct
indistinguishable

adv indistinguish-
ably

individual

adv individually

individualism
individualist
individuality
indivisible
indoctrinate
indoctrinated
indoctrinating
indolence
indolent
indomitable

adv indomitably

indoor
indoors
indubitable

adv indubitably

induce
induced
inducing
inducement
induct
induction
inductive
indulge
indulged
indulging
indulgence
industrial

*an industrial process:
an industrial worker
(= in industry)*

industrialist
industrious

*an industrious child
(= hardworking)*

inebriated
inebriation
inedible

ineffable

adv ineffably

ineffective

adv ineffectively

ineffectiveness
ineffectual

adv ineffectually

inefficiency
inefficient
inelegance
inelegant
ineligibility
ineligible

*ineligible for the
post because of lack
of qualifications*

inept

*an inept attempt:
an inept young man*

ineptitude
inequality

pl inequalities

inert
inertia
inescapable

adv inescapably

inestimable

adv inestimably

inevitability
inevitable

adv inevitably

inexcusable

adv inexcusably

inexhaustible
inexorable

adv inexorably

inexpensive

adv inexpensively

inexperience

inexperienced
inexplicable
    adv inexplicably
inexpressible
    adv inexpressibly
inextricable
    adv inextricably
infallibility
infallible
    adv infallibly
infamous
infamy
infancy
infant
infanticide
infantry
infatuated
infatuation
infect
infection
infectious
infer
   inferred
   inferring
inference
inferior
inferiority
infernal
    adv infernally
inferno
    pl infernos
infertile
infertility
infest
infidel
infidelity
infiltrate
   infiltrated
   infiltrating

infiltration
infinite
    adv infinitely
infinitesimal
    adv
      infinitesimally
infinitive
infinity
infirm
infirmary
    pl infirmaries
infirmity
    pl infirmities
inflame
   inflamed
   inflaming
inflammable
   Petrol is highly
   inflammable
inflammation
inflammatory
inflate
   inflated
   inflating
inflation
inflationary
inflection see
   inflexion
inflexible
inflexion,
   inflection
inflict
infliction
influence
   influenced
   influencing
influential
    adv influentially
influenza

influx
inform
informal
    adv informally
informality
informant
information
informative
    adv informatively
informer
infra-red
infringe
   infringed
   infringing
infringement
infuriate
   infuriated
   infuriating
infuse
   infused
   infusing
infusion
ingenious
    an ingenious idea
ingenuity
ingenuous
    young and ingenuous
ingenuousness
ingot
ingrained
ingratiate
   ingratiated
   ingratiating
ingratitude
ingredient
inhabit
   inhabited
   inhabiting
inhabitant

inhalant
inhalation
inhale
  inhaled
  inhaling
inherent
inherit
  inherited
  inheriting
inheritance
inhibit
  inhibited
  inhibiting
inhibition
inhospitable
  adv inhospitably
inhuman

*The torturing of
prisoners is inhuman:
a strange,
inhuman laugh*

inhumane

*inhumane treatment
of animals*

  adv inhumanely
inimical
  adv inimically
inimitable
  adv inimitably
iniquitous
iniquity
  pl iniquities
initial
  initialled
  initialling
initially
initiate
  initiated
  initiating

initiation
initiative
inject
injection
injudicious
injunction
injure
  injured
  injuring
injury
  pl injuries
injustice
ink
inkling
inky
inlaid *see* inlay
inland
inlay
  inlaid
  inlaying
inlet
inmate
inmost
inn

to stay at an inn

innate
inner
innings
innkeeper
innocence
innocent
innocuous
innovation
innuendo
  pl innuendoes
innumerable
innumeracy
innumerate
inoculate

inoculated
inoculating
inoculation
inoffensive
  adv inoffensively
inopportune
  adv
    inopportunely
inordinate
  adv inordinately
inorganic
in-patient
input
inquest
inquire, enquire
  inquired,
    enquired
  inquiring,
    enquiring
inquirer, enquirer
inquiry, enquiry
  pls inquiries,
    enquiries
inquisition
inquisitive
  adv inquisitively
inquisitor
inroads
insane
  adv insanely
insanitary
insanity
insatiable
  adv insatiably
inscribe
  inscribed
  inscribing
inscription
inscrutable

adv inscrutably
insect
insecticide
insecure
  adv insecurely
insecurity
insensible
insensitive
  adv insensitively
inseparable
  adv inseparably
insert
insertion
inset
inshore
inside
insidious
insight
insignia
insignificance
insignificant
insincere
  adv insincerely
insincerity
insinuate
  insinuated
  insinuating
insinuation
insipid
insist
insistence
insistent
insolence
insolent
insoluble
insolvent
insomnia
insomniac
inspect

inspection
inspector
inspiration
inspire
  inspired
  inspiring
instability
instal, install
  installed
  installing
installation
instalment
instance
instant
instantaneous
instead
instep
instigate
  instigated
  instigating
instigation
instil
  instilled
  instilling
instinct
instinctive
  adv instinctively
institute
  instituted
  instituting
institution
institutional
instruct
instruction
instructive
  adv instructively
instructor
instrument
instrumental

instrumentalist
insubordinate
insubordination
insufferable
  adv insufferably
insufficiency
insufficient
insular
insulate
  insulated
  insulating
insulation
insulin
insult
insuperable
  adv insuperably
insurance
insure
  to insure one's life:
  to insure one's house
  against theft
insured
insuring
insurgence
insurgent
insurmountable
  adv
    insurmountably
insurrection
intact
intake
intangible
  adv intangibly
integral
integrate
  integrated
  integrating
integration
integrity

intellect
intellectual
  adv intellectually
intelligence
intelligent
  bright and intelligent
intelligible
  *a scarcely
  intelligible account
  of the accident*

  adv intelligibly
intemperance
intemperate
  adv intemperately
intend
intense
  adv intensely
intensify
  intensified
  intensifying
intensity
intensive
  adv intensively
intent
intentional
  adv intentionally
inter
  interred
  interring
interact
interaction
intercede
  interceded
  interceding
intercept
intercession
interchange
  interchanged
  interchanging

interchangeable
intercom
intercourse
interdict
interest
interesting
interfere
  interfered
  interfering
interference
interim
interior
interject
interjection
interlock
interloper
interlude
intermediary
  pl intermediaries
intermediate
interment
  *the interment
  of the corpse*
interminable
  adv interminably
intermission
intermittent
intern
internal
  adv internally
international
  adv
    internationally
internee
internment
  *the internment
  of the prisoner*
interpret
  interpreted

interpreting
interpretation
interpreter
interrogate
  interrogated
  interrogating
interrogation
interrogative
interrogator
interrupt
interruption
intersection
intersperse
  interspersed
  interspersing
interstice
interval
intervene
  intervened
  intervening
intervention
interview
intestate
intestinal
intestines
intimacy
intimate
  adv intimately
  intimated
  intimating
intimation
intimidate
  intimidated
  intimidating
intimidation
into
intolerable
  adv intolerably
intolerance

intolerant
intonation
intone
  intoned
  intoning
intoxicant
intoxicate
  intoxicated
  intoxicating
  intoxication
intractable
intransigence
intransigent
intransitive
intrusive
  adv intrusively
intrepid
intrepidity
intricacy
  pl intricacies
intricate
  adv intricately
intrigue
  intrigued
  intriguing
intrinsic
  adv **intrinsically**
introduce
  introduced
  introducing
introduction
introductory
introspection
introspective
  adv
    introspectively
intrude
  intruded
  intruding

intruder
intrusion
intrusive
intuition
intuitive
  adv intuitively
inundate
  inundated
  inundating
  inundation
inure
  inured
  inuring
invade
  invaded
  invading
invader
invalid
invalidate
  invalidated
  invalidating
invalidity
invaluable
  adv **invaluably**
invariable
  adv **invariably**
invasion
invective
inveigle
  inveigled
  inveigling
invent
invention
inventive
inventor
inventory
  pl inventories
inverse
  adv inversely

inversion
invert
invertebrate
  *A worm is an
  invertebrate creature*
invest
investigate
  investigated
  investigating
investigation
investigator
investiture
investment
investor
inveterate
  an inveterate liar
invidious
invigilate
  invigilated
  invigilating
invigilator
invigorate
  invigorated
  invigorating
invincible
inviolable
inviolate
invisibility
invisible
  adv invisibly
invitation
invite
  invited
  inviting
invocation
invoice
invoke
  invoked
  invoking

involuntary
  adv involuntarily
involve
  involved
  involving
involvement
inward
inwardly
inwards
iodine
iota
IOU
irascibility
irascible
  adv irascibly
irate
  adv irately
ire
iridescence
iridescent
iris
  pl irises
Irish
irk
irksome
iron
  ironed
  ironing
ironic, ironical
  adv ironically
ironmonger
irony
  pl ironies
irrational
  adv irrationally
irregular
irregularity
  pl irregularities
irrelevance

irrelevancy
irrelevant
irreparable
  adv irreparably
irreplaceable
irrepressible
  adv irrepressibly
irreproachable
  adv
    irreproachably
irresistible
  adv irresistibly
irresolute
  adv irresolutely
irrespective
  adv irrespectively
irresponsible
  adv
    irresponsibly
irreverence
irreverent
irrevocable
  adv irrevocably
irrigate
  irrigated
  irrigating
irrigation
irritable
  adv irritably
irritant
irritate
  irritated
  irritating
irritation
is *see* be
island
islander
isle
  Isle of Man

isn't
  = is not
isobar
isolate
  isolated
  isolating
isolation
isosceles
isotherm
issue
  issued
  issuing
isthmus
  pl isthmuses
it
Italian
italicize, -ise
  italicized
  italicizing
italics
itch
  pl itches
itchy
item
itinerant
itinerary
  pl itineraries
it'll
  = it shall, it will
it's
  = it is
  It's fine
its
  its leg
itself
I've
  = I have
ivory
ivy

J

jab
  jabbed
  jabbing
jabber
  jabbered
  jabbering
jack
jackal
jackass
  pl jackasses
jackdaw
jacket
jack-in-the-box
jack-knife
jackpot
jade
jaded
jag
  jagged
  jagging
jaguar
jail, gaol
  *He was sent
  to jail/gaol*
jailer, gaoler
jam
  *strawberry jam: in a
  jam: Did the machine
  jam?: to jam full*
  jammed
  jamming
jamb
  the door jamb
jamboree
jangle
  jangled
  jangling
116

janitor
January
jar
  jarred
  jarring
jargon
jasmine
jaundice
jaunt
jaunty
  adv jauntily
javelin
jaw
jay
jaywalker
jazz
jealous
jealousy
jeans
jeep
jeer
  jeered
  jeering
jelly
  pl jellies
jellyfish
jeopardize, -ise
  jeopardized
  jeopardizing
jeopardy
jerboa
jerk
jerkin
jerky
  adv jerkily
jersey
  pl jerseys
jest
jester

jet
jetsam
jettison
  jettisoned
  jettisoning
jetty
  pl jetties
Jew
  a Jew from Israel
  pl Jews
  Jews in the synagogue
jewel
jeweller, jeweler
jewellery, jewelry
Jewish
jib
  *to jib at paying
  a lot*
  jibbed
  jibbing
jibe, gibe
  to sneer and jibe
  jibed, gibed
  jibing, gibing
jig
  jigged
  jigging
jigsaw
jilt
jingle
  jingled
  jingling
job
  jobbing
jockey
  pl jockeys
  jockeyed
  jockeying
jocular

jocularity
jodhpurs
jog
  jogged
  jogging
joggle
  joggled
  joggling
join
  joined
  joining
joiner
joint
joist
joke
  joked
  joking
joker
jollification
jollity
jolly
  compar jollier
  superl jolliest
  adv jollily
jolt
joss-stick
jostle
  jostled
  jostling
jot
  jotted
  jotting
jotter
joule
journal
journalism
journalist
journey
  pl journeys

journeyed
journeying
joust
jovial
  adv jovially
jowl
joy
joyful
  adv joyfully
joyfulness
joyless
joyous
jubilant
jubilation
jubilee
judge
  judged
  judging
judgement,
  judgment
judicial
  a judicial inquiry
judiciary
judicious
  a judicious choice
  of books
judo
jug
  jugged
juggernaut
juggle
  juggled
  juggling
juggler
jugular (vein)
juice
juicy
ju-jitsu
jukebox

July
jumble
  jumbled
  jumbling
jumble-sale
jumbo
jump
jumper
jumpy
junction
  a road junction
juncture
  at this juncture
June
jungle
junior
juniper
junk
junket
junketing
jurisdiction
juror
jury
  pl juries
just
justice
justifiable
  adv justifiably
justification
justify
  justified
  justifying
jut
  jutted
  jutting
jute
juvenile
juxtapose
  juxtaposed

117

juxtaposing
juxtaposition

K

kaftan, caftan
kaiser
kale
kaleidoscope
kaleidoscopic
 adv kaleidoscopi-
 cally
kangaroo
 pl kangaroos
kapok
karate
kart
 a go-kart
kayak
kebab
kedgeree
keel
 keeled
 keeling
keelhaul
keen
keenness
keep
 kept
 keeping
keeper
keepsake
keg
kelp
kelvin
kennel
kept *see* keep
kerb

She stood on the kerb
kernel
kerosene
kestrel
ketch
 pl ketches
ketchup
kettle
key
 the key to the door
keyboard
keyed-up
keyhole
keynote
khaki
kibbutz
 pl kibbutzim
kick
kick-off
kid
kidnap
 kidnapped
 kidnapping
kidnapper
kidney
 pl kidneys
kill
killer
kiln
kilogramme
kilometre
kilowatt
kilt
kimono
 pl kimonos
kin
kind
kindergarten
kindle

kindled
kindling
kindliness
kindly
kindness
kindred
kinetic
 adv kinetically
king
kingdom
kingfisher
kingly
kink
kinky
kinsman
kiosk
kipper
kiss
 pl kisses
kit
kitchen
kitchenette
kite
kitten
kittiwake
kitty
kiwi
 pl kiwis
kleptomania
kleptomaniac
knack
knacker
knackered
knapsack
knave
 the knave of hearts
knavish
knead
 knead the bread

knee
  kneed
    *He kneed him in
    the stomach*
  kneeing
kneel
  knelt
  kneeling
knell
knelt *see* kneel
knew *see* know
knickerbockers
knickers
knick-knack
knife
  pl knives
  knifed
  knifing
knight
  *a knight in
  shining armour*
knighted
knighthood
knightly
  *Bravery is a
  knightly quality*
knit
  to knit a cardigan
  knitted
  knitting
knob
knock
knocker
knock-kneed
knoll
knot
  a knot in the string
  knotted
  knotting

knotty
  a knotty problem
know
  I know her well
  knew
  I knew it
  known
  I should have known
  knowing
knowingly
knowledge
knowledgeable
  adv
  knowledgeably
known *see* know
knuckles
knuckle under
  knuckled under
  knuckling under
koala bear
kookaburra
Koran
kosher
kowtow
  kowtowed
  kowtowing
kudos
kung-fu

L

lab
label
  labelled
  labelling
laboratory
  pl **laboratories**
laborious
labour

laboured
labouring
labourer
laburnum
labyrinth
lace
  laced
  lacing
lacerate
  lacerated
  lacerating
laceration
lack
lackadaisical
  adv
  lackadaisically
lackey
  pl lackeys
laconic
  adv laconically
lacquer
  lacquered
  lacquering
lacrosse
lactic
lad
ladder
  laddered
  laddering
lade
  a mill lade
laden
ladies *see* lady
lading
ladle
  ladled
  ladling
lady
  pl ladies

ladybird
ladyship
lag
  lagged
  lagging
lager
lagoon
laid *see* lay
lain *see* lie
lair
  a wolf's lair
laird
laity
lake
lama
  *Tibetans respect
  the lama*
lamb
lame
lameness
lament
lamentable
lamentation
lamp
lance
  lanced
  lancing
lance-corporal
land
landau
landlady
  pl landladies
landlord
landscape
lane
  a country lane
language
languid
languish

languor
languorous
  adv languorously
laniard *see*
  lanyard
lank
lanky
lantern
lanyard, laniard
lap
  lapped
  lapping
lapdog
lapel
lapidary
  pl lapidaries
lapse
  lapsed
  lapsing
lapwing
larceny
larch
  pl larches
lard
larder
large
largely
largeness
largesse
lariat
lark
larkspur
larva
  pl larvae
laryngitis
larynx
lascivious
laser
lash

pl lashes
lass
  pl lasses
lassitude
lasso
  pl lassos, lassoes
last
lastly
latch
  pl latches
latchkey
late
lately
latency
lateness
latent
lateral
  adv laterally
  A crab moves laterally
latex
lath
  a lath of wood
lathe
  *A mechanic
  uses a lathe*
lather
lathered
lathering
Latin
latitude
latter
latterly
  *Latterly he has
  grown senile*
lattice
laud
  lauded
  lauding
laudable

adv laudably
laugh
laughable
  adv laughably
laughter
launch
  pl launches
launder
  laundered
  laundering
launderette
laundry
  pl laundries
laurel
lava
lavatory
  pl lavatories
lavender
lavish
law
lawful
  adv lawfully
lawless
lawlessness
lawn
lawnmower
lawyer
lax
laxative
laxity
lay see lie
lay
  to lay it on the table
  laid
  She laid it on the bed
  laying
layabout
layby
  pl laybys

layer
  two layers of cloth
layette
laze
  lazed
  lazing
laziness
lazy
  compar lazier
  superl laziest
  adv lazily
lea
  the green lea
lead [lĕd]
  to lead into battle
  led
  He led me to the king
  leading
lead [lĕd]
  lead pipes
leaden
leader
leaf
  pl leaves
leaflet
leafy
league
leak
  a gas leak:
  Does this kettle leak?
leakage
lean
  leant, leaned
  leaning
leanness
·leant see lean
leap
  leapt, leaped
  leaping

leapfrog
leapt see leap
learn
  learned, learnt
  learning
learner
lease
  leased
  leasing
leasehold
leash
  pl leashes
least see little
leather
  leathered
  leathering
leathery
leave
  left
  leaving
leaves see leaf
leavings
lecherous
lechery
lectern
lecture
  lectured
  lecturing
lecturer
led see lead
ledge
ledger
lee
  in the lee of the boat
leech
  pl leeches
leek
  leek soup
leer

121

leered
leering
lees
leeward
leeway
left *see* leave
leg
legacy
  pl legacies
legal
  adv legally
legality
  pl legalities
legalize, -ise
  legalized
  legalizing
legatee
legation
legend
legendary
legerdemain
leggings
leggy
legibility
legible
  clear, legible writing
  adv legibly
legion
legionary
legislate
  legislated
  legislating
legislation
legislative
legislator
legislature
legitimacy
legitimate
  adv legitimately

leisure
leisured
leisurely
lemming
  *like lemmings to
  the sea*
lemon
  an orange and a lemon
lemonade
lemony
lemur
lend
  lent
  lending
length
lengthen
  lengthened
  lengthening
lengthways
lengthy
  adv lengthily
leniency
lenient
lens
  pl lenses
Lent
lent *see* lend
lentil
leopard
  a tiger and a leopard
leotard
leper
  *a leper dressed
  in rags*
leprechaun
leprosy
less *see* little
lessen
  to lessen the pain

lessened
lessening
lesser
lesson
  a French lesson
lest
let
  let
  letting
lethal
lethargic
  adv lethargically
lethargy
letter
lettered
lettering
lettuce
leukaemia
levee
level
  levelled
  levelling
lever
leveret
leviathan
levied *see* levy
levitate
  levitated
  levitating
levitation
levity
levy
  pl levies
  levied
  levying
lewd
lewdness
lexicographer
lexicography

liability
  pl liabilities
liable
  *You are liable to slip
  on ice: liable for
  her debts*
liaise
  liaised
  liaising
liaison
liar
  Don't believe a liar
libel
  *guilty of libel:
  Did the newspaper
  libel him?*

  libelled
  libelling
libellous
liberal
  adv liberally
liberality
liberate
  liberated
  liberating
liberation
libertine
liberty
  pl liberties
librarian
library
  pl libraries
libretto
  pl libretti,
  librettos
lice *see* louse
licence
  *a dog licence:
  poetic licence*

license
  to license a dog
  licensed
  licensing
licensee
licentious
licentiousness
lichen
lick
lid
lie
  lied
  He lied about his age
  lying
lie
  lay
  He lay down
  lain
  *He has lain down:
  He'd lain there
  for three days*
  lying
liege
lieu
lieutenant
life
  pl lives
lifeguard
lifeless
life-like
lift
lift-off
ligament
ligature
light
  lit, lighted
  lighting
lighten
  lightened

lightening
  lightening the load
lighter
lighthouse
lightning
  thunder and lightning
like
  liked
  liking
likeable, likable
likelihood
likely
likeness
likewise
lilac
lilt
lily
  pl lilies
limb
limber
  limbered
  limbering
limbo
lime
limelight
limit
  limited
  limiting
limitation
limousine
limp
limpet
limpid
linchpin
line
  lined
  lining
lineage
lineal

adv lineally
lineament
  the lineaments
  of her face
linear
linen
liner
linesman
linger
  lingered
  lingering
lingerie
linguist
linguistic
  adv linguistically
linguistics
liniment
  to rub some liniment
  on his leg
lining
link
links
linnet
lino
linoleum
linseed
lint
lintel
lion
lioness
  pl lionesses
lionize, -ise
  lionized
  lionizing
lip
lipstick
liquefy
  liquefied
  liquefying
124

liqueur
  Cointreau is an
  orange liqueur
liquid
liquidate
  liquidated
  liquidating
liquidation
liquidator
liquor
  whisky and other
  strong liquors
liquorice
lisp
lissom, lissome
list
listen
  listened
  listening
listener
listless
lit *see* light
litany
  pl litanies
literacy
literal
  a literal translation
  adv literally
literary
  He has literary tastes
literate
  He is scarcely
  literate
literature
lithe
lithograph
litigation
litre
litter

littered
littering
little
  compar less
  superl least
liturgical
liturgy
  pl liturgies
live [liv]
  lived
  living
live [liv]
livelihood
liveliness
livelong
lively
  compar livelier
  superl liveliest
liven up
  livened up
  livening up
liver
livery
  pl liveries
livestock
livid
living
living-room
lizard
llama
  The llama is of
  the camel family
lo!
load
  a load of coal:
  to load the lorry
  with coal
loaf
  pl loaves

loaf
  loafed
  loafing
loam
loan
  a book on loan
loath, loth
  I am loath to go
loathe
  I loathe cruelty
  loathed
  loathing
lob
  lobbed
  lobbing
lobby
  pl lobbies
lobe
lobster
local
  local people:
  drinking in his local
locale
  the locale of the film
locality
localize, -ise
  localized
  localizing
locate
  located
  locating
location
loch
lock
locker
locket
lockjaw
locomotion
locomotive

locum
  pl locums
locust
lode
  A lode is a vein in
  rock containing metal
lodestar
lodestone
lodge
  lodged
  lodging
lodger
loftiness
lofty
  adv loftily
log
  logged
  logging
loganberry
  pl loganberries
logbook
loggerheads
logic
logical
  adv logically
loin
loincloth
loiter
  loitered
  loitering
loll
  lolled
  lolling
lone
  a lone cottage:
  a lone star
loneliness
lonely
lonesome

long
longevity
longing
longitude
loo
look
lookout
loom
  loomed
  looming
loop
  looped
  The pilot looped
  the loop
  looping
loophole
loose
  a loose-fitting coat:
  This screw is loose:
  a loose woman
  adv loosely
loosen
loosened
  loosening
loot
  the burglar's loot
lop
  lopped
  He lopped a branch
  from the tree
  lopping
lope
  loped
  The large dog
  loped along
  loping
lopped *see* lop
lop-sided
loquacious

lord
lordly
lordship
lore
lorgnette
lorry
  pl lorries
lose
  to lose a glove:
  to lose weight:
  to lose time

lost
losing
loser
loss
  pl losses
lost see lose
lot
loth see loath
lotion
lottery
  pl lotteries
lotus
loud
loudness
loudspeaker
lounge
  lounged
  lounging
lour see lower
louse
  pl lice
lout
lovable
love
  loved
  loving
loveliness
lovely
126

compar lovelier
superl loveliest
lover
low
lower ['lōər]
  lowered
  lowering
lower, lour ['lowər]
lowland
lowliness
lowly
lowness
loyal
  adv loyally
loyalist
loyalty
lozenge
lubricant
lubricate
  lubricated
  lubricating
lubrication
lucid
lucidity
luck
lucky
  compar luckier
  superl luckiest
  adv luckily
lucrative
lucre
ludicrous
ludo
lug
  lugged
  lugging
luggage
lugubrious
lukewarm

lull
  lulled
  lulling
lullaby
  pl lullabies
lumbago
lumbar
  lumbar pain
lumber
  rubbish and lumber:
  Elephants lumber
  through the forests:
  to lumber him
  with the work

lumbered
lumbering
lumberjack
luminosity
luminous
lump
lumpy
lunacy
lunar
lunatic
lunch
  pl lunches
luncheon
lung
lunge
  lunged
  lunging
lupin
lurch
lure
  lured
  luring
lurid
lurk
luscious

lush
lust
lustful
  adv lustfully
lustre
lustrous
lusty
  adv lustily
lute
  to play a lute
luxuriant
luxuriate
  luxuriated
  luxuriating
luxurious
luxury
  pl luxuries
lying see lie
lymph gland
lynch
lynx
  pl lynxes
lyre
  A lyre is like a harp
lyrebird
lyric
lyrical
  adv lyrically

M

macabre
macaroni
  macaroni cheese
macaroon
  biscuits and
  macaroons
macaw
mace

machete
machination
machine
machinery
machinist
Mach number
mackerel
mackintosh
  pl mackintoshes
mad
  compar madder
  superl maddest
madam
madden
  maddened
  maddening
made see make
Madeira
madman
  pl madmen
madness
Madonna
madrigal
maelstrom
maestro
  pl maestros
magazine
magenta
maggot
maggoty
magic
magical
  adv magically
magician
magisterial
magistrate
magnanimity
magnanimous
magnate

He is a shipping
magnate
magnesia
magnesium
magnet
  A magnet attracts
  iron
magnetic
  adv magnetically
magnetism
magnetization,
  -isation
magnetize, -ise
  magnetized
  magnetizing
magnification
magnificence
magnificent
magnify
  magnified
  magnifying
magnitude
magnolia
magpie
Maharajah
mahogany
maid
  a chamber-maid
maiden
mail
  first-class mail:
  mail the letter
  mailed
  mailing
maim
  maimed
  maiming
main
  the main points of

127

his speech
mainland
mainly
mainsail
mainstay
maintain
maintaining
maintained
maintenance
maize
fields of maize
majestic
adv majestically
majesty
pl majesties
major
majority
pl majorities
make
made
She made a cake
making
maker
makeshift
make-up
maladjusted
malady
pl maladies
malaise
malapropism
malaria
male
male and female
malevolence
malevolent
malformation
malformed
malice
malicious

malign
maligned
maligning
malignant
malinger
malingered
malingering
malingerer
mallard
malleable
mallet
malnutrition
malodorous
malpractice
malt
maltreat
maltreatment
mamma, mama
mammal
mammoth
man
pl men
manned
manning
manacle
manage
managed
managing
manageable
management
manager
manageress
mandarin
mandate
mandatory
mandible
mandoline,
   mandolin
mane

a horse's mane
manful
adv manfully
mange
manger
mangle
mangled
mangling
mango
pl mangoes
mangy
manhandle
manhandled
manhandling
manhood
mania
maniac
*The murderer was
a maniac*
maniacal
manic
a manic depressive
manicure
manicurist
manifest
manifestation
manifesto
pl manifestos,
   manifestoes
manifold
manipulate
manipulated
manipulating
manipulation
mankind
manna
manned *see* man
mannequin
manner

a manner of speaking:
a pleasant manner

mannerism
mannerly
mannish
manoeuvre
manor
  the lord of the manor
manorial
manpower
manse
mansion
manslaughter
mantelpiece
mantilla
mantle
manual
  adv manually
manufacture
  manufactured
  manufacturing
manufacturer
manure
manuscript
Manx cat
many
map
  mapped
  mapping
maple
mar
  marred
  marring
maraud
marauder
marauding
marble
marcasite
March

march
  pl marches
marchioness
  pl marchionesses
mare
  a mare and her foal
margarine
margin
marginal
  adv marginally
marguerite
marigold
marijuana
marina
  yachts in the marina
marine
mariner
marionette
marital
maritime
marjoram
mark
marked
marker
market
  marketed
  marketing
marmalade
maroon
  marooned
  marooning
marquee
marquess,
  marquis
  pls marquesses,
  marquises
marriage
marriageable
marrow

marry
married
marrying
marsh
  pl marshes
marshal
  an air marshal:
  a US marshal:
  to marshal the troops
marshalled
marshalling
marshmallow
marshy
marsupial
martello tower
marten
  the fur of a marten
martial
  martial music:
  martial law
martin
  a martin's nest
martinet
martyr
martyred
martyring
martyrdom
marvel
  marvelled
  marvelling
marvellous
marzipan
mascot
masculine
masculinity
mash
mask
  The surgeon wore
  a mask: The burglar

wore a mask
masochism
masochist
masochistic
  adv
    masochistically
mason
masonic
masonry
masque
  The minstrels took part in the masque
masquerade
  masqueraded
  masquerading
  masquerader
mass
  pl masses
massacre
  massacred
  massacring
massage
  massaged
  massaging
masseur
masseuse
massive
mast
master
masterful
  adv masterfully
masterliness
masterly
masterpiece
mastery
masticate
  masticated
  masticating
mastication

mastiff
masturbate
  masturbated
  masturbating
mat *see* matt
mat
  a mat by the front door: This material tends to mat
matted
matting
matador
match
  pl matches
matchbox
  pl matchboxes
matchless
mate
  mated
  mating
material
  adv materially
materialism
materialistic
  adv
    materialistically
materialization,
  -isation
materialize, -ise
  materialized
  materializing
maternal
  adv maternally
maternity
mathematical
  adv
    mathematically
mathematician
mathematics

matinee
matins
matricide
matriculate
  matriculated
  matriculating
matriculation
matrimonial
matrimony
matron
matronly
matt, matte, mat
  matt paint
matter
mattered
  mattering
matter-of-fact
mattress
  pl mattresses
mature
  matured
  maturing
maturity
maudlin
maul
  mauled
  mauling
mausoleum
mauve
mawkish
maxim
maximum
  pl maxima
May
may
  might
maybe
mayday
mayonnaise

130

mayor
the Lord Mayor of London

mayoress

maypole

maze
lost in a maze

me

mead

meadow

meagre
adv **meagrely**

meal

mean
a mean old miser: What does the word mean?

meant

meaning

meander
meandered
meandering

meaning

meaningful
adv meaningfully

meaningless

meanness

meant *see* mean

meanwhile

measles

measly

measure
measured
measuring

measurement

meat
Vegetarians don't eat meat

meaty

mechanic

mechanical
adv **mechanically**

mechanics

mechanism

mechanization, -isation

mechanize, -ise
mechanized
mechanizing

medal
a gold medal

medallion

medallist

meddle
to meddle in people's affairs

meddled
meddling

meddler

media *see* medium

mediaeval, medieval

mediate
to mediate in a dispute

mediated
mediating

mediation

mediator

medical
adv medically

medicated

medication

medicinal

medicine

medieval *see* mediaeval

mediocre

mediocrity

meditate
to pray and meditate

meditated

meditating

meditation

meditative

medium
pl media
the mass media
pl mediums
Mediums are psychic

medley
pl medleys

meek

meerschaum

meet
They meet in the church hall

met

meeting

megalomania

megaphone

megaton

melancholic

melancholy

mellifluous

mellow

melodic

melodious

melodrama

melodramatic
adv melodramatically

melody
pl melodies

melon

melt

member
membership
membrane
memento
  pl mementos
memo
memoir
memorable
  adv memorably
memorandum
  pl memoranda
memorial
memorize, -ise
  memorized
  memorizing
memory
  pl memories
men *see* man
menace
  menaced
  menacing
ménage
menagerie
mend
mendacious
mendacity
mendicant
menial
meningitis
menstrual
menstruate
  menstruated
  menstruating
menstruation
mental
  adv mentally
mentality
  pl mentalities
menthol

mention
mentioned
mentioning
mentor
menu
  pl **menus**
mercantile
mercenary
  pl mercenaries
merchandise
merchant
merciful
  adv mercifully
merciless
mercurial
mercury
mercy
mere
  adv merely
merge
  merged
  merging
merger
meridian
meringue
merino
  merino wool
merit
  merited
  meriting
meritorious
mermaid
merman
merriment
merry
  compar merrier
  superl merriest
  adv merrily
merry-go-round

merrymaking
mesh
  pl meshes
mesmerism
mesmerize, -ise
  mesmerized
  mesmerizing
mess
  pl messes
message
messenger
met *see* meet
metal
  a metal box
metallic
metallurgical
metallurgy
metamorphosis
  pl metamor-
    phoses
metaphor
metaphorical
  adv
    metaphorically
meteor
meteoric
meteorite
meteorological
  adv meteorolo-
    gically
meteorologist
meteorology
mete out
  to mete out
  punishment
meted out
meting out
meter
  a gas meter

method
methodical
  adv methodically
methylated spirits
meticulous
metre
  a metre of cloth
metric
metrical
metricate
  metricated
  metricating
metrication
metronome
metropolis
  pl metropolises
metropolitan
mettle
  *That horse has plenty
  of mettle*
mew
mews
  a mews flat
mezzo-soprano
miaow
mica
mice *see* mouse
Michaelmas daisy
microbe
microcosm
microfilm
microphone
microprocessor
microscope
microscopic
midday
middle
middle-aged
middle-class

middling
midge
midget
midnight
midriff
midst
midway
midwife
  pl midwives
midwifery
mien
  a solemn mien
might *see* may
might
  the might of the army
mightiness
mighty
  compar mightier
  superl mightiest
  adv mightily
migraine
migrant
migrate
  migrated
  migrating
migratory
mike
mild
mildew
mile
mileage
milestone
milieu
militant
military
militate
  militated
  militating
militia

milk
milky
mill
millennium
  pl millennia
miller
millet
milligramme
millilitre
millimetre
milliner
millinery
million
millionaire
millstone
mime
  mimed
  miming
mimic
mimicked
  mimicking
mimicry
mimosa
minaret
mince
  minced
  mincing
mincemeat
mincer
mind
mindful
mindless
mine
miner
  a coal miner
mineral
mineralogical
  adv
  mineralogically

mineralogist
mineralogy
mingle
  mingled
  mingling
mini
  pl minis
miniature
minibus
  pl minibuses
minimal
minimize, -ise
  minimized
  minimizing
minimum
  pl minima
minion
minister
  a minister of the
  church: to minister
  to her needs

  ministered
  ministering
ministerial
  adv ministerially
ministry
  pl ministries
mink
minnow
minor
  of minor importance:
  legally, a minor
minority
  pl minorities
minster
  York Minster
minstrel
mint
minuet
134

minus
minute
minx
  pl minxes
miracle
miraculous
mirage
mire
mirror
  mirrored
  mirroring
mirth
misadventure
misanthropist
misanthropy
misbehave
  misbehaved
  misbehaving
  misbehaviour
miscarriage
miscarry
  miscarried
  miscarrying
miscellaneous
miscellany
  pl miscellanies
mischance
mischief
mischievous
misconception
misconduct
miscreant
misdeed
misdemeanour
miser
miserable
  adv miserably
miserly
misery

  pl miseries
misfire
  misfired
  misfiring
misfit
misfortune
misgiving
misguided
mishap
mislay
  mislaid
  mislaying
mislead
  misled
  misleading
misnomer
misogynist
misprint
miss
  pl misses
  missed
  missing
missal
  The choirboy carried
  a missal

misshapen
missile
  a nuclear missile
mission
missionary
  pl missionaries
missive
misspell
  misspelled,
  misspelt
  misspelling
misspent
mist
mistake

mistaken
We were mistaken
mistook
I mistook her for you
mistaking
mister
mistletoe
mistook *see*
mistake
mistress
pl mistresses
mistrust
misty
misunderstand
misunderstood
misunderstanding
misuse
mite
a poor little mite
mitigate
mitigated
mitigating
mitigation
mitre
mitt
mitten
mix
pl mixes
mixer
mixture
mnemonic
moan
moaned
moaning
moat
*a moat round
the castle*
mob
mobbed

mobbing
mobile
mobility
mobilization,
-isation
mobilize, -ise
mobilized
mobilizing
moccasin
mock
mockery
mocking
modal
a modal verb
mode
model
a model aeroplane
modelled
modelling
moderate
adv moderately
moderation
moderator
modern
modernity
modernization,
-isation
modernize, -ise
modernized
modernizing
modest
modesty
modicum
modification
modify
modified
modifying
modish
modulate

modulated
modulating
modulation
module
a space module
mohair
Mohammedan
moist
moisten
moistened
moistening
moisture
moisturize, -ise
moisturized
moisturizing
molar
molasses
mole
molecular
molecule
molehill
molest
mollify
mollified
mollifying
mollusc
mollycoddle
mollycoddled
mollycoddling
molten
moment
momentary
a momentary pause
adv momentarily
momentous
*a momentous
discovery*
momentum
to gather momentum

monarch
monarchy
  pl monarchies
monastery
  pl monasteries
monastic
monasticism
Monday
monetary
money
moneyed, monied
mongoose
  pl mongooses
mongrel
monitor
  monitored
  monitoring
monk
monkey
  pl monkeys
  monkeyed
  monkeying
monocle
monogamous
monogamy
monogram
monologue
monopolize, -ise
  monopolized
  monopolizing
monopoly
  pl monopolies
monosyllabic
monosyllable
monotone
monotonous
monotony
monsoon
monster

monstrosity
  pl monstrosities
monstrous
month
monthly
  pl monthlies
monument
monumental
moo
mood
moody
moon
moonbeam
moonlight
moor
  moored
  mooring
  moorings
moose
  the antlers of a moose
  pl moose
moot point
mop
  mopped
  She mopped the floor
  mopping
mope
  moped
  She moped and sulked
  moping
moped ['mōped]
mopped *see* mop
moral
  the moral of the story
  adv morally
morale
  *Morale was low in
  the army*
morality

goodness and morality
moralize, -ise
  moralized
  moralizing
morass
  pl morasses
morbid
morbidity
more
moreover
morgue
moribund
morn
morning
moron
moronic
morose
  adv morosely
morphia
morris dance
morrow
morse
morsel
mortal
  adv mortally
mortality
  *the mortality rate
  in car crashes*
mortar
mortgage
  mortgaged
  mortgaging
mortice *see*
  mortise
mortification
mortify
  mortified
  mortifying
mortise, mortice

mortuary
  pl mortuaries
mosaic
Moslem
mosque
mosquito
  pl mosquitos,
    mosquitoes
moss
  pl mosses
mossy
most
mostly
mote
  a mote in the eye
moth
mothball
moth-eaten
mother
  mothered
  mothering
  motherhood
mother-in-law
  pl mothers-in-
    law
  motherliness
  motherly
motif
  a motif of flowers
motion
motionless
motivate
  motivated
  motivating
motive
  a motive for murder
motley
motor
motor-bike

motorcycle
motorist
motorize, -ise
  motorized
  motorizing
motorway
mottled
motto
  pl mottoes
mould
moulder
mouldering
mouldy
moult
mound
mount
mountain
mountaineer
mountainous
mountebank
mourn
mourner
mournful
  adv mournfully
mourning
mouse
  The cat ate the mouse
  pl mice
mousse
  lemon mousse
moustache
mousy
mouth
  mouthed
  mouthing
mouthful
  pl mouthfuls
movable,
  moveable

move
moved
moving
movement
movie
  pl movies
moving
mow
mowed
mowing
mower
Mr
Mrs
Ms
much
muck
mucous
  a mucous substance
mucus
  mucus from the nose
muddle
muddled
muddling
muddy
mudguard
muff
muffin
muffle
muffled
muffling
muffler
mufti
mug
mugged
mugging
mugger
muggy
mulatto
  pl mulattos

mulberry
  pl mulberries
mulch
mule
mulish
mull
mullet
multi-coloured
multifarious
multimillionaire
multinational
multiple
  multiple injuries:
  8 is a multiple of 4
multiplication
multiplicity
multiply
  × is the sign
  for multiply
multiplied
multiplying
multitude
multitudinous
mumble
  mumbled
  mumbling
mummify
  mummified
  mummifying
mummy
  pl mummies
mumps
munch
mundane
municipal
municipality
  pl municipalities
munificence
munificent

munitions
mural
murder
  murdered
  murdering
  murderer
  murderous
murky
murmur
  murmured
  murmuring
muscle
  well-developed
  muscles
muscular
muse
  to muse on the beauty
  of nature
  mused
  musing
museum
  pl museums
mush
mushroom
  mushroomed
  mushrooming
mushy
music
musical
  adv musically
musician
musk
musket
musketeer
Muslim
musquash
mussel
  I love fresh mussels
must

mustard
muster
  mustered
  mustering
musty
mute
muted
mutilate
  mutilated
  mutilating
mutilation
mutineer
mutinous
mutiny
  pl mutinies
  mutinied
  mutinying
mutter
  muttered
  muttering
mutton
mutual
  adv mutually
muzzle
  muzzled
  muzzling
muzzy
my
myopia
myopic
  adv myopically
myriad
myrrh
myrtle
myself
mysterious
mystery
  pl mysteries
mystic

mystic philosophy
adv mystically
mystify
  mystified
  mystifying
mystique
  the mystique of the stage
myth
mythical
  adv mythically
mythological
mythology
myxomatosis

N

nadir
nag
  nagged
  nagging
naiad
nail
  nailed
  nailing
naive
naiveté
naked
namby-pamby
name
  named
  naming
namely
nanny
  pl nannies
nap
  napped
  napping
nape

naphtha
napkin
nappy
  pl nappies
narcissus
  pl narcissi
narcotic
narrate
  narrated
  narrating
narration
narrative
narrator
narrow
nasal
nastiness
nasturtium
nasty
  adv nastily
natal
nation
national
  adv nationally
nationalism
nationality
  pl nationalities
nationalization, -isation
nationalize, -ise
  nationalized
  nationalizing
native
nativity
natty
  adv nattily
natural
  adv naturally
naturalist
naturalize, -ise

naturalized
naturalizing
nature
naught
  He cared naught for her
naughtiness
naughty
  a naughty child
  adv naughtily
nausea
nauseate
  nauseated
  nauseating
nauseous
nautical
naval
  a naval battle
nave
  the nave of a church
navel
  The baby's navel has healed
navigable
navigate
  navigated
  navigating
navigation
navigator
navvy
  a navvy on a building site
  pl navvies
navy
  to join the navy
  pl navies
nay
  Nay, he will not come
near

nearly
nearness
neat
nebulous
necessary
  adv necessarily
necessitate
  necessitated
  necessitating
necessity
  pl necessities
neck
necklace
necromancy
necropolis
  pl necropolises
nectar
nectarine
née
  Ann Smith née Jones
need
  Animals need water
needful
needle
needless
needy
ne'er
ne'er-do-well
nefarious
negate
  negated
  negating
negative
neglect
neglectful
negligée
negligence
negligent
  a careless, negligent

  mother
negligible
  a negligible amount
  adv negligibly
negotiable
negotiate
  negotiated
  negotiating
negotiation
negotiator
negro
  pl negroes
negroid
neigh
  to neigh like a horse
neighed
neighing
neighbour
neighbourhood
neighbouring
neighbourliness
neighbourly
neither
nemesis
neologism
neon lighting
nephew
nerve
nervous
nervousness
nervy
nest
nestle
  nestled
  nestling
net, nett
  nett profit
net
  a ball in the net:

  to net a fish
netted
netting
netball
nether
nethermost
nett see net
nettle
network
neuralgia
neurosis
neurotic
neuter
  neutered
  neutering
neutral
  adv neutrally
neutrality
neutralize, -ise
  neutralized
  neutralizing
neutron
never
nevertheless
new
  a new dress
newfangled
newly
newness
news
newsagent
newspaper
newt
next
nib
nibble
  nibbled
  nibbling
nice

adv nicely
nicety
pl niceties
niche
nick
nickel
nickname
nicotine
niece
niggardly
niggling
nigh
night
a cold, dark night
nightdress
nightfall
nightingale
nightly
a new show nightly
nightmare
nil
nimble
adv nimbly
nimbus
nincompoop
nine
nineteen
nineteenth
ninetieth
ninety
ninny
ninth
nip
nipped
nipping
nipple
nit
a stupid nit:
nits in her hair

nitrate
nitric
nitrogen
nitwit
no
We have no money:
She answered 'No'
pl noes
nobility
noble
adv nobly
nobody
nocturnal
adv nocturnally
nod
nodded
nodding
node
nodule
Noël, Nowell
noise
noisy
adv **noisily**
nomad
nomadic
nom de plume
pl noms de
plume
nomenclature
nominal
adv nominally
nominate
nominated
nominating
nomination
nominee
= a person who
has been
nominated

nonagenarian
nonchalance
nonchalant
non-committal
nonconformist
nondescript
none
nonentity
pl nonentities
nonplussed
nonsense
nonsensical
adv nonsensically
noodle
nook
no-one
noose
nor
norm
normal
adv normally
north
northerly
in a northerly
direction
northern
northern lands
Norwegian
nose
nosey, nosy
nostalgia
nostalgic
adv nostalgically
nostril
not
He is not here
notability
pl notabilities
notable

141

adv **notably**
notary public
  pl notaries public
notation
notch
  pl notches
note
  noted
  noting
noteworthy
nothing
nothingness
notice
  noticed
  noticing
noticeable
  adv **noticeably**
notifiable
notification
notify
  notified
  notifying
notion
notoriety
notorious
notwithstanding
nougat ['noogä]
  This nougat is sticky
nought
  *The telephone number
  contains two noughts*
noun
nourish
nourishment
novel
novelist
novelty
  pl novelties
November

novice
now
nowadays
Nowell *see* Noël
nowhere
noxious
nozzle
nuance
nuclear
nucleus
  pl nuclei
nude
nudist
nudity
nudge
  nudged
  nudging
nugget
  a gold nugget
nuisance
null
nullify
  nullified
  nullifying
numb
number
  numbered
  numbering
numeracy
numeral
numerate
numerical
  adv numerically
numerous
numismatics
numskull
nun
nunnery
  pl nunneries

nuptial
nurse
  nursed
  nursing
nursery
  pl nurseries
nurture
  nurtured
  nurturing
nut
nutcracker
nutmeg
nutrient
nutriment
nutrition
nutritious
nutshell
nutty
nuzzle
  nuzzled
  nuzzling
nylon
nymph

O

o, oh
oaf
  pl oafs
oak
oar
  an oar for a boat
oasis
  pl oases
oath
  pl oaths
oats
obduracy
obdurate

adv obdurately
obedience
obedient
obeisance
obelisk
obese
obesity
obey
  obeyed
  obeying
obituary
  pl obituaries
object
objection
objectionable
  adv objectionably
objective
  adv objectively
obligation
obligatory
  adv obligatorily
oblige
  obliged
  obliging
oblique
obliterate
  obliterated
  obliterating
oblivion
oblivious
oblong
obnoxious
oboe
  pl oboes
oboist
obscene
  adv obscenely
obscenity
  pl obscenities

obscure
  adv obscurely
obscurity
obsequious
observance
observant
observation
observatory
  pl observatories
observe
  observed
  observing
observer
obsess
obsession
obsessive
  adv obsessively
obsolescent
obsolete
obstacle
obstetrical
obstetrician
obstetrics
obstinacy
obstinate
  adv obstinately
obstreperous
obstruct
obstruction
obtain
  obtained
  obtaining
obtainable
obtrusive
  adv obtrusively
obtuse
  adv obtusely
obviate
  obviated

obviating
obvious
obviously
occasion
occasional
  adv **occasionally**
occult
occupancy
occupant
occupation
occupier
occupy
  occupied
  occupying
occur
  occurred
  occurring
occurrence
ocean
oceanic
ochre
octagonal
  adv octagonally
octave
octet
October
octogenarian
octopus
  pl octopuses
ocular
oculist
odd
oddity
  pl oddities
oddment
ode
odious
odium
odour

odourless

of

a cup of tea:
made of silver:
to die of hunger

off

to switch off a light:
to run off:
to finish off a job:
badly off:
The meat is off

offal
off-chance
offence
offend
offender
offensive
 adv offensively
offer
 offered
 offering
offhand
office
officer
official
 official action:
 official duties
 adv officially
officiate
 officiated
 officiating
officious
 rude and officious
offing
off-licence
offset
 offset
 offsetting
offshoot

offside
offspring
oft
often
ogle
 ogled
 ogling
ogre
oh *see* o
oil
 oiled
 oiling
oilfield
oilrig
oily
ointment
OK
okay
 okayed
 okaying
old
old-fashioned
olive
ombudsman
omega
omelette, omelet
omen .
ominous
omission
 He apologized for
 the omission of her
 name from the list
omit
 omitted
 omitting
omnibus
 pl omnibuses
omnipotent
omniscient

omnivorous
on
once
oncoming
one
onerous
oneself
ongoing
onion
onlooker
only
onslaught
onus
onwards
onyx
ooze
 oozed
 oozing
opacity
opal
opaque
open
 opened
 opening
opener
openly
opera *see* opus
opera
operate
 operated
 operating
operatic
operation
operative
operator
operetta
ophthalmic
ophthalmologist
opiate

opinion
opinionated
opium
opossum
opponent
opportune
opportunism
opportunist
opportunity
  pl opportunities
oppose
  opposed
  opposing
opposite
opposition
oppress
oppression
oppressive
opprobrious
opprobrium
opt
optical
optician
optimism
optimist
optimistic
  adv optimistically
optimum
option
optional
  adv optionally
opulence
opulent
opus
  pl opera
or
oracle
oral
  The dentist spoke

about oral hygiene
  adv orally
orange
orang-utan
oration
orator
oratorio
  pl oratorios
oratory
  pl oratories
orb
orbit
  orbited
  orbiting
orchard
orchestra
orchid
ordain
ordeal
order
  ordered
  ordering
orderly
  pl orderlies
ordinal
ordinance
ordinary
  adv ordinarily
ordination
Ordnance Survey
ore
  iron ore
organ
organdie
organic
  adv organically
organism
  *This poison kills all
  known organisms*

organist
organization,
  -isation
organize, -ise
  organized
  organizing
orgasm
  sexual orgasm
orgy
  pl orgies
orient
oriental
orientate
  orientated
  orientating
orienteering
orifice
origin
original
  adv originally
originate
  originated
  originating
ornament
ornamental
  adv ornamentally
ornate
ornithological
ornithologist
ornithology
orphan
orphanage
orthodox
orthodoxy
orthography
orthopaedic
oscillate
  oscillated
  oscillating

145

oscillation
osprey
  pl ospreys
ostensible
  adv ostensibly
ostentation
ostentatious
osteopath
ostracism
ostracize, -ise
  ostracized
  ostracizing
ostrich
  pl ostriches
other
otter
ottoman
ought
ounce
our
ours
ourselves
oust
out
outboard
outbreak
outcast
outcome
outcry
outdo
  outdid

  *She outdid
  her neighbours*

  outdone

  She has outdone them

  outdoing
outdoor
outer
outermost

outfit
outfitter
outing
outlandish
outlaw
outlay
outlet
outline
outlook
outlying
outnumber
  outnumbered
  outnumbering
out-patient
output
outrage
outrageous
outright
outset
outside
outsize
outskirts
outspoken
outstanding
outward
outwit
  outwitted
  outwitting
oval
ovary
  pl ovaries
ovation
oven
over
overall
overawe
  overawed
  overawing
overbearing

overcame *see*
  overcome
overcoat
overcome
  overcame

  *He overcame his
  enemies*

  overcome

  He has overcome them

  overcoming
overdo
  overdid

  She overdid the meat

  overdone

  She has overdone it

  overdoing
overdose
overdraft
overdrawn
overflow
overgrown
overheads
overhear
  overheard
  overhearing
overjoyed
overlap
  overlapped
  overlapping
overlook
overpowering
overran *see*
  overrun
overrate
  overrated
  overrating
overreach
overrun
  overran

The enemy overran the country

overrun

They have overrun the country

overrunning
overseas
overseer
overshadow
oversight
overstep
  overstepped
  overstepping
overt
overtake
  overtook
  He overtook the car
  overtaken
  He has overtaken the car
  overtaking
overthrow
  overthrew
  He overthrew the king
  overthrown
  He has overthrown the king
  overthrowing
overtime
overtook *see* overtake
overture
overwhelm
overwrought
owe
  owed
  owing
owl
own

owned
owning
owner
ox
  pl oxen
oxygen
oyster
ozone

P

pace
  paced
  pacing
pacifist
pacify
  pacified
  pacifying
pack
  packed
  *We packed the cases:
  a packed hall*
  packing
package
packed *see* pack
packet
pact
  a pact between nations
pad
  padded
  padding
paddle
  paddled
  paddling
paddock
padlock
pagan
page
  paged

paging
pageant
pageantry
pagoda
paid *see* pay
pail
  a pail of water
pain
  a pain in his chest
pained
painful
  adv painfully
painless
painstaking
paint
painter
painting
pair
  a pair of shoes
paired
pairing
pal
palace
palatable
palate
  *the soft palate
  of the mouth*
palatial
palaver
pale
  *thin and pale:
  of a pale colour*
palette
  an artist's palette
palindrome
paling
palisade
pall
  palled

147

palling
pallet
  a straw pallet
palliative
pallid
pallor
palm
palmist
palmistry
palpable
  adv palpably
palpitation
palsy
paltry
pampas
pamper
  pampered
  pampering
pamphlet
pan
  panned
  panning
panacea
panache
pancake
panda
pandemonium
pander
  pandered
  pandering
pane
  a pane of glass
panegyric
panel
panelling
pang
panic
  panicked
  panicking

pannier
panoply
panorama
pansy
  pl pansies
pant
pantechnicon
panther
pantomime
pantry
  pl pantries
pants
papa
papacy
papal
paper
  papered
  papering
paperback
paperweight
papier mâché
papoose
paprika
papyrus
par
  *not up to par: on a par
  with his brother*
parable
parachute
parachutist
parade
  paraded
  parading
paradise
paradox
  pl paradoxes
paradoxical
  adv paradoxically
paraffin

paragon
paragraph
parakeet
parallel
parallelogram
paralyse
  paralysed
  paralysing
paralysis
paralytic
paramount
paramour
parapet
paraphernalia
paraphrase
paraplegia
paraplegic
parasite
parasitic
parasol
paratrooper
paratroops
parboil
  parboiled
  parboiling
parcel
  parcelled
  parcelling
parch
parchment
pardon
  pardoned
  pardoning
pardonable
pare
  *to pare an apple: to
  pare one's toenails*
pared
paring

parent
parentage
parental
parenthesis
  pl parentheses
parenthetical
pariah
parish
  pl parishes
parishioner
parity
park
parka
parley
  pl parleys
parleyed
parleying
parliament
parliamentary
parlour
parlourmaid
parochial
parody
  pl parodies
parodied
parodying
parole
paroxysm
parquet
parr
  A parr is a
  young salmon
parrot
parry
  parried
  parrying
parse
  parsed
  parsing

parsimonious
parsimony
parsley
parsnip
parson
parsonage
part
partake
  partook
  partaken
  partaking
partial
  adv **partially**
partiality
participant
participate
  participated
  participating
participation
participle
particle
particular
particularly
partisan
partition
partly
partner
  partnered
  partnering
partook *see*
  partake
partridge
party
  pl parties
pass
  passed
  He passed out of
  sight: The bus passed
  the house: The feeling

soon passed

passing
passable
passage
passed *see* pass
passenger
passer-by
  pl **passers-by**
passion
passionate
  adv **passionately**
passive
  adv **passively**
passport
password
past
  The old think about
  the past: We walked
  past the church

pasta
paste
pastel
  pastel colours
pasteurization,
  -isation
pasteurize, -ise
  pasteurized
  pasteurizing
pastille
  a throat pastille
pastime
pastor
pastoral
pastry
  pl pastries
pasturage
pasture
pasty [ˈpāsti]

pasty ['pasti]
  pl pasties
pat
  patted
  patting
patch
  pl patches
patchwork
patchy
pate
  a bald pate
pâté
  pâté on toast
patent
patently
paternal
  adv paternally
paternity
path
pathetic
  adv pathetically
pathological
pathologist
pathology
pathos
patience
patient
patio
  pl patios
patois
patriarch
patriarchal
patricide
patriot
patriotic
  adv patriotically
patriotism
patrol
  patrolled
150

patrolling
patron
patronage
patronize, -ise
  patronized
  patronizing
patter
  pattered
  pattering
pattern
patterned
patty
  a mince patty
  pl patties
paucity
paunch
  pl paunches
pauper
pause
  paused
  pausing
pave
  paved
  paving
pavement
pavilion
paw
pawn
pawnbroker
pay
  paid
  paying
payable
payee
  = the person to
  whom money
  is paid
payment
pea

peace
  peace and quiet
peaceable
  adv **peaceably**
peaceful
  adv peacefully
peach
  pl peaches
peacock
peak
  a mountain peak
peaky
peal
  a peal of bells:
  Bells peal
  pealed
  pealing
peanut
pear
  an apple and a pear
pearl
  a pearl necklace
peasant
  a simple peasant
peat
pebble
pebbly
pecan
peccadillo
  pl peccadillos,
    peccadilloes
peck
peckish
peculiar
peculiarity
  pl peculiarities
pecuniary
pedal
  to pedal a bicycle

pedalled
pedalling
pedant
pedantic
  adv pedantically
peddle
  to peddle one's wares
peddled
peddling
pedestal
pedestrian
pedigree
pedigreed
pedlar
pedometer
peek
  *a peek through
  the window*
peel
  to peel an apple
peeled
peeling
peep
peeped
peeping
peer
  *to peer through the
  window: a peer of
  the realm*
peered
peering
peerage
peerless
peevish
peewit
peg
pegged
pegging
pejorative

Pekinese,
  Pekingese
pelican
pellet
pell-mell
pelmet
pelt
pelvis
pen
  penned
  penning
penal
penalize, -ise
  penalized
  penalizing
penalty
penance
pence *see* penny
pencil
  pencilled
  pencilling
pendant
  a silver pendant
pendent
  a pendent light
pending
pendulum
penetrate
  penetrated
  penetrating
penetration
pen-friend
penguin
penicillin
peninsula
penis
penitent
penitentiary
penknife

pen-name
pennant
pennies *see*
  penny
penniless
penny
  pl pence
  This costs ten pence
  pl pennies
  *This machine takes
  pennies*
pension
pensioner
pensive
  adv pensively
pentagon
pentathlon
penthouse
pent-up
penultimate
penury
peony
  pl peonies
people
  peopled
  peopling
pepper
  peppered
  peppering
peppercorn
peppermint
peppery
pep-talk
perambulator
perceive
  perceived
  perceiving
per cent
percentage

perceptible
  adv perceptibly
perception
perceptive
perch
  pl perches
percolate
  percolated
  percolating
percolator
percussion
perdition
peremptory,
  adv peremptorily
perennial
  adv perennially
perfect
perfection
perfectionist
perfidious
perfidy
perforate
  perforated
  perforating
perform
performance
performer
perfume
perfunctory
  adv perfunctorily
perhaps
peril
perilous
perimeter
period
periodic
  adv **periodically**
periodical
peripatetic
152

peripheral
periphery
  pl peripheries
periscope
perish
perishable
periwinkle
perjure
  perjured
  perjuring
perjury
perk
perky
perm
permanence
permanency
permanent
permeable
permeate
  permeated
  permeating
permissible
permission
permissive
permissiveness
permit
  permitted
  permitting
permutation
pernicious
pernickety
peroxide
perpendicular
perpetrate
  perpetrated
  perpetrating
perpetrator
perpetual
  adv perpetually

perpetuate
  perpetuated
  perpetuating
perpetuity
perplex
perplexity
  pl perplexities
perquisite
  A company car is one
  of the perquisites
  of the job

persecute
  persecuted
  persecuting
persecution
persecutor
perseverance
persevere
  persevered
  persevering
persist
persistence
persistent
person
personable
personal
  She is his personal
  assistant: a personal
  letter

  adv personally
personality
  pl personalities
personification
personify
  personified
  personifying
personnel
  the company's
  personnel officer

perspective
Perspex ®
perspicacious
perspicacity
perspiration
perspire
  perspired
  perspiring
persuade
  persuaded
  persuading
persuasion
persuasive
  adv persuasively
pert
pertain
  pertained
  pertaining
pertinacious
pertinacity
pertinence
pertinent
perturb
perturbation
perusal
peruse
  perused
  perusing
pervade
  pervaded
  pervading
perverse
  adv perversely
perversion
perversity
pervert
peseta
pessimism
pessimist

pessimistic
  adv
    pessimistically
pest
pester
  pestered
  pestering
pesticide
pestilence
pestle
pet
  petted
  petting
petal
peter out
  petered out
  petering out
petite
petition
petrel
  a gull and a petrel
petrify
  petrified
  petrifying
petrol
  two gallons of petrol
petroleum
petticoat
pettiness
petty
  adv pettily
petulance
petulant
pew
pewter
phantom
Pharaoh
  pl Pharaohs
pharmaceutical

pharmacist
pharmacological
pharmacologist
pharmacology
pharmacy
  pl pharmacies
pharyngitis
pharynx
phase
  phased
  phasing
pheasant
  pheasant feathers
phenomenal
phenomenon
  pl phenomena
phial
philander
  philandered
  philandering
  philanderer
philanthropic
  adv philanthropi-
    cally
philanthropist
philanthropy
philatelist
philately
philosopher
philosophic
  adv
    philosophically
philosophy
phlegm
phlegmatic
phlox
  *phlox growing in
  the garden*
phobia

153

pl phobias
phobic
phoenix
phone
phonetics
phoney, phony
phosphate
phosphorescent
phosphorous
photocopy
  photocopied
  photocopying
photogenic
  adv
    photogenically
photograph
photographer
photographic
  adv photographi-
    cally
photography
phrase
  phrased
  phrasing
phraseology
physical
  adv physically
physician
physicist
physics
physiological
  adv
    physiologically
physiologist
physiology
physiotherapist
physiotherapy
physique
pianist

piano
  pl pianos
piazza
  a church in the piazza
pibroch
piccolo
  pl piccolos
pick
picket
  picketed
  picketing
pickle
  pickled
  pickling
pick-pocket
picnic
  picnicked
  picnicking
pictorial
  adv pictorially
picture
picturesque
  adv picturesquely
pie
piebald
piece
  a piece of paper
piecemeal
piecework
pied
pier
  the pier at
  the seaside
pierce
  pierced
  piercing
pierrot
piety
piffle

pig
pigeon
pigeon-hole
piggery
pigment
pigmentation
pigmy see pygmy
pigsty
pigtail
pike
pilchard
pile
  piled
  piling
pilfer
  pilfered
  pilfering
pilgrim
pilgrimage
pill
pillage
pillar
pillion
pillory
  pl pillories
  pilloried
  pillorying
pillow
pilot
  piloted
  piloting
pimpernel
pimple
pimply
pin
  pinned
  flowers pinned
  to her dress
  pinning

154

pinafore
pince-nez
pincers
pinch
  pl pinches
pinched
pine
  pined
  The dog pined and died
  pining
pineapple
ping
ping-pong
pinion
  pinioned
  pinioning
pink
pinnacle
pinned *see* pin
pint
pioneer
  pioneered
  pioneering
pious
pip
  pipped
  He was pipped
  at the post
  pipping
pipe
  piped
  a cake piped with
  white icing: The
  members of the band
  piped away all night

  piping
pipeline
piper
pipette

pipped *see* pip
piquancy
piquant
pique
  to resign out of
  pique: to pique one's
  curiosity

  piqued
  piquing
piracy
pirate
pirouette
  pirouetted
  pirouetting
pistachio
  pl **pistachios**
pistil
  the pistil of a flower
pistol
  shot by a pistol
piston
pit
  pitted
  pitting
pitch
  pl pitches
pitcher
piteous
pitfall
pith
pithy
pitiable
pitiful
  adv pitifully
pittance
pity
  pitied
  pitying
pivot

pivoted
pivoting
pixie, pixy
  pl pixies
pizza
  a tomato and cheese
  pizza
placard
placate
  placated
  placating
place
  a place in the sun:
  to place the book
  on the table

  placed
  placing
placid
plagiarism
plagiarize, -ise
  plagiarized
  plagiarizing
plague
plaice
  plaice and chips
plaid
plain
  Wheat grows on the
  plain: a plain dress

plaintiff
  The plaintiff lost
  the case

plaintive
  a plaintive cry
plait
  to plait hair
  plaited
  plaiting
plan

planned
planning
plane

The plane landed:
The joiner uses a
plane: a plane-tree:
a plane surface

planet
planetary
plank
plankton
plant
plantation
planter
plaque
plasma
plaster
  plastered
  plastering
plasterer
plastic
Plasticine ®
plasticity
plate

a plate of food:
to plate with silver

  plated
  plating
plateau
  pl plateaux,
    plateaus
platform
platinum
platitude
platonic
platoon
platter
platypus
  pl platypuses

plaudit
plausibility
plausible
  adv plausibly
play
  played
  playing
player
playful
  adv playfully
playmate
playschool
playwright
plea
plead
pleasant
pleasantness
pleasantry
  pl pleasantries
please
  pleased
  pleasing
pleasurable
  adv pleasurably
pleasure
pleat
  pleated
  pleating
plebeian
plebiscite
plectrum
pledge
  pledged
  pledging
plenary
plenteous
plentiful
  adv plentifully
plenty

plethora
pleurisy
pliable
pliant
pliers
plight
plimsoll
plod
  plodded
  plodding
plop
  plopped
  plopping
plot
  plotted
  plotting
plough
  ploughed
  ploughing
plover
pluck
plucky
  adv pluckily
plug
  plugged
  plugging
plum

a red plum

plumage
plumb

to plumb the depths

  plumbed
  plumbing
plumber
plumbline
plume
plummet
plump
plunder

plundered
plundering
plunge
  plunged
  plunging
plural
plus
plush
plutocrat
plutocratic
ply
  plied
  plying
plywood
pneumatic
  adv
    pneumatically
pneumonia
poach
poacher
pocket
  pocketed
  pocketing
pockmark
pod
podgy
poem
poet
poetic
  adv poetically
poetry
poignance
poignant
point
pointed
pointer
pointless
poise
poised

poison
poisonous
poke
  poked
  poking
poker
poky
polar
pole
polecat
police
  policed
  policing
policeman
  pl policemen
policy
  pl policies
polio
poliomyelitis
polish
  pl polishes
polite
  adv politely
politeness
politic
  It is politic to do
  as the king says
political
  a political figure
  adv politically
politician
politics
polka
poll
  polled
  polling
pollen
pollinate
  pollinated

pollinating
pollination
pollute
  polluted
  polluting
pollution
polo
poltergeist
polygamist
polygamous
polygamy
polyglot
polygon
polysyllabic
polytechnic
polythene
pomegranate
pommel
pomp
pompous
poncho
  pl ponchos
pond
ponder
  pondered
  pondering
ponderous
pontiff
pontificate
  pontificated
  pontificating
pontoon
pony
  pl ponies
pony-trekking
poodle
pool

  a swimming pool:
  football pools: to

pool their resources
pooled
pooling
poop
poor
poorly
pop
popped
popping
pope
poplar
*a poplar and
a yew tree*
poplin
poppy
pl poppies
populace
popular
a popular entertainer
popularity
popularize, -ise
popularized
popularizing
populate
populated
populating
population
populous
porcelain
porch
pl porches
porcupine
pore
a blocked pore
pored
*He pored
over his books*
poring
pork

pornographic
pornography
porous
porpoise
porridge
port
portable
portal
portcullis
pl portcullises
portend
portent
portentous
porter
portfolio
pl portfolios
port-hole
portico
pl porticos,
porticoes
portion
portly
portmanteau
pl portmanteaux,
portmanteaus
portrait
portray
portrayed
portraying
portrayal
pose
posed
posing
poser
*a poser before the
camera: That question
is quite a poser*

poseur
He is a poseur

and a sham
posh
position
positioned
positioning
positive
adv positively
posse
possess
possessed
possessing
possession
possessive
adv possessively
possessor
possibility
pl possibilities
possible
adv possibly
post
postage
postal
postcard
poster
posterior
posterity
postern
posthumous
postmortem
postpone
postponed
postponing
postponement
postscript
postulate
postulated
postulating
posture
postwar

158

posy
 pl posies
pot
  potted
  potting
potash
potassium
potato
 pl **potatoes**
potency
potent
potential
 adv potentially
pothole
potholing
potion
pot-pourri
potter
  pottered
  pottering
pottery
 pl potteries
pouch
 pl pouches
pouffe
poultice
poultry
pounce
  pounced
  pouncing
pound
pour
  Did the rain pour down?
poured
  She poured milk from the jug
pouring
pout

pouted
pouting
poverty
powder
  powdered
  powdering
powdery
power
  powered
powerful
 adv powerfully
powerless
pow-wow
practicable
  It is not practicable to try to make the journey in one day

practical
  a practical knowledge of carpentry: He is a dreamer but his wife is very practical

practically
practice
  She is at dancing practice: a doctor's practice

practise
  You must practise your dance steps
  practised
  practising
practitioner
pragmatic
pragmatist
prairie
praise
  praised
  praising

pram
prance
  pranced
  prancing
prank
prattle
  prattled
  prattling
prawn
pray
  I heard the minister pray
  prayed
  praying
prayer
preach
preacher
preamble
prearrange
  prearranged
  prearranging
precarious
precaution
precautionary
precede
  She always precedes him into the room
  preceded
  preceding
precedence
precedent
precept
precinct
precious
precipice
precipitate
  precipitated
  precipitating
precipitous

159

précis
pl précis
precise
adv precisely
precision
preclude
precluded
precluding
precocious
precocity
preconception
precursor
predator
predatory
predecessor
predicament
predict
predictable
adv predictably
prediction
predilection
predominant
pre-eminent
preen
preened
preening
prefabricated
preface
prefect
prefer
preferred
preferring
preferable
preference
preferential
preferment
prefix
pl prefixes
pregnancy

pl pregnancies
pregnant
prehistoric
adv
prehistorically
prejudge
prejudged
prejudging
prejudice
prejudiced
prejudicing
prejudicial
prelate
preliminary
pl preliminaries
prelude
premature
adv prematurely
premeditated
premier
Who is the Italian premier?
première
the première of the play
premise
pl premises
false premises
premises
They moved to new premises
premium
pl premiums
premonition
preoccupation
preoccupied
prepaid *see*
prepay
preparation

preparatory
prepare
prepared
preparing
prepay
prepaid
prepaying
prepayment
preponderance
preposition
prepossessing
preposterous
prerequisite
Patience is a prerequisite for teaching
prerogative
presage
presaged
presaging
Presbyterian
prescribe
prescribed
prescribing
prescription
prescriptive
presence
present
presentable
adv presentably
presentation
presentiment
presently
preservation
preservative
preserve
preserved
preserving
preside

presided
presiding
presidency
president
press
pressgang
pressure
pressurize, -ise
pressurized
pressurizing
prestige
prestigious
presumably
presume
presumed
presuming
presumption
presumptuous
pretence
pretend
pretender
pretension
pretentious
preternatural
adv
preternaturally
pretext
prettiness
pretty
adv prettily
prevail
prevailed
prevailing
prevalence
prevalent
prevaricate
prevaricated
prevaricating
prevarication

prevent
preventive
preview
previous
previously
prey
Mice are prey for owls: Owls prey on mice
preyed
preying
price
What is the price of that house?: I would price that hat at £5
priced
pricing
priceless
prick
prickle
prickled
prickling
prickly
pride
prided
priding
priest
priesthood
priggish
prim
prima donna
primarily
primary
primate
prime
primed
priming
primer
primeval

primitive
adv primitively
primrose
prince
princely
princess
pl princesses
principal
the principal of the college
principality
pl principalities
principally
principle
the principle of the steam engine: a man of principle
print
printer
prior
prioress
pl prioresses
priority
pl priorities
priory
pl priories
prise
to prise open a lid
prised
prising
prism
prison
prisoner
pristine
privacy
private
private information: a private secretary
adv privately

privateer
privation
privet
a privet hedge
privilege
privileged
privy council
prize
to win a prize: to prize a possession dearly

prized
prizing
probability
pl probabilities
probable
adv **probably**
probation
probe
probed
probing
probity
problem
problematic
proboscis
pl proboscises
procedure
proceed
Proceed on your way!
proceeded
proceeding
proceeds
process
pl processes
processed
processing
procession
proclaim
proclamation
162

procrastinate
procrastinated
procrastinating
procrastination
procurator fiscal
procure
procured
procuring
prod
prodded
prodding
prodigal
prodigious
prodigy
pl prodigies
produce
produced
producing
producer
product
production
productive
adv productively
productivity
profane
adv profanely
profanity
profess
profession
professional
adv
professionally
professor
proffer
proffered
proffering
proficiency
proficient
profile

profit
profit and gain
profited
profiting
profitable
adv profitably
profiteer
profiteered
profiteering
profligacy
profligate
profound
profuse
adv profusely
profusion
progenitor
progeny
prognosticate
prognosticated
prognosticating
prognostication
program
a computer program: to program a computer

programmed
programming
programme
a theatre programme

progress
progression
progressive
adv progressively
prohibit
prohibited
prohibiting
prohibition
prohibitive
adv prohibitively
project

projectile
projection
projector
proletarian
proletariat
proliferate
  proliferated
  proliferating
prolific
prolix
prolixity
prologue
prolong
promenade
prominence
prominent
promiscuity
promiscuous
promise
  pl promises
  promised
  promising
promontory
  pl promontories
promote
  promoted
  promoting
promotion
prompt
  adv promptly
prone
prong
pronoun
pronounce
  pronounced
  pronouncing
pronouncement
pronunciation
proof

*Do they have proof of
his guilt?: 70% proof
spirit*

prop
  propped
  propping
propaganda
propagandist
propagate
  propagated
  propagating
  propagator
propel
  propelled
  propelling
propeller
propensity
  pl propensities
proper
properly
property
  *the lost property
  office*
  pl properties
prophecy
  to make a prophecy
  pl prophecies
prophesy
  *to prophesy about
  the future*
  prophesied
  prophesying
prophet
  *an Old Testament
  prophet*
propinquity
propitiate
  propitiated
  propitiating

proportion
proportional
  adv
  proportionally
proportionate
  adv
  proportionately
proposal
propose
  proposed
  proposing
proposition
propound
proprietor
proprietress,
  proprietrix
propriety
  *She behaved with
  dignity and propriety*
  pl proprieties
propulsion
prosaic
  adv prosaically
prose
prosecute
  prosecuted
  prosecuting
prosecution
prospect
prospective
prospector
prospectus
  pl prospectuses
prosper
  prospered
  prospering
prosperity
prosperous
prostate

163

the prostate gland
prostitute
prostrate
*to prostrate
with grief: He lay
prostrate on the floor*

prostrated
prostrating
prostration
protagonist
protect
protection
protective
adv protectively
protector
protégé
protein
protest
Protestant
protestation
protocol
proton
prototype
protract
protractor
protrude
protruded
protruding
protrusion
protuberance
protuberant
proud
prove
*Can you prove that he
murdered her?*

proved
proving
provender
proverb

proverbial
adv proverbially
provide
provided
providing
providence
provident
providential
adv providentially
province
provincial
adv provincially
provision
provisional
adv provisionally
proviso
pl provisos
provocation
provocative
adv provocatively
provoke
provoked
provoking
prow
prowess
prowl
prowler
proximity
proxy
pl proxies
prude
prudence
prudent
prudery
prudish
prune
pruned
pruning
pry

pried
prying
psalm
psalter
pseudo
pseudonym
psychiatric
psychiatrist
psychiatry
psychic
psychoanalysis
psychological
adv
psychologically
psychologist
psychology
ptarmigan
pterodactyl
pub
puberty
pubic
public
adv **publicly**
publican
publication
publicity
publish
publisher
puce
pucker
puckered
puckering
pudding
puddle
puerile
puff
puffin
puffy
pugilist

pugnacious
pugnacity
pull
to pull a cart
pullet
pulley
pl pulleys
pullover
pulmonary
pulp
pulpit
pulsate
pulsated
pulsating
pulse
pulsed
pulsing
pulverize, -ise
pulverized
pulverizing
puma
pumice stone
pummel
pummelled
pummelling
pump
pumpkin
pun
punned
punning
punch
pl punches
punctilious
punctual
adv punctually
punctuality
punctuate
punctuated
punctuating

punctuation
puncture
punctured
puncturing
pundit
pungent
punish
punishable
punishment
punitive
punnet
punt
puny
pup
pupa
pl pupae
pupil
puppet
puppy
pl puppies
purchase
purchased
purchasing
purchaser
pure
purée
purely
purgative
purgatory
purge
purged
purging
purification
purify
purified
purifying
purist
puritan
puritanical

adv puritanically
purity
purl
knit one, purl one
purled
purling
purloin
purple
purport
purpose
purposeful
adv purposefully
purposely
purr
purred
purring
purse
purser
pursue
pursued
pursuing
pursuer
pursuit
pus
push
pushy
pusillanimous
put
*to put a cup on
the table*
put
putting
putative
putrefaction
putrefy
putrified
putrefying
putrid
putt

165

to putt a ball
putted
putting
putter
putty
puzzle
puzzled
puzzling
pygmy, pigmy
pl pygmies,
pigmies
pyjamas
pylon
pyramid
pyre
Pyrex ®
Pyrrhic
python

Q

quack
quad
quadrangle
quadrangular
quadrant
quadrilateral
quadrille
quadruped
quadruple
quadruplet
quaff
quail
quailed
quailing
quaint
quake
quaked
quaking

qualification
qualify
qualified
qualifying
qualitative
quality
pl qualities
qualm
quandary
pl quandaries
quantitative
quantity
pl quantities
quarantine
quarrel
quarrelled
quarrelling
quarrelsome
quarry
pl quarries
quarried
quarrying
quart
quarter
quarterly
quartet
quartz
quasar
quash
to quash a rebellion
quasi-
quaver
quavered
quavering
quay
*the boat tied to
the quay*
queasiness
queasy

adv queasily
queen
queenly
queer
quell
quench
querulous
query
pl queries
queried
querying
quest
question
questioned
questioning
questionable
adv questionably
questionnaire
queue
*a cinema queue: to
queue for the cinema*
queued
queuing,
queueing
quibble
quibbled
quibbling
quick
quicken
quickened
quickening
quickness
quid
quiescent
quiet
a shy, quiet child
quieten
quietened
quietening

166

quietness
quill
quilt
quilted
quin
quince
quinine
quinquennial
quintessence
quintessential
quintet
quintuplet
quip
  quipped
  quipping
quire
  a quire of paper
quirk
quit
  quitted, quit
  quitting
quite
  quite pretty
quiver
  quivered
  quivering
quixotic
  adv quixotically
quiz
  pl quizzes
  quizzed
  quizzing
quizzical
  adv quizzically
quoits
quorum
quota
  pl quotas
quotation

quote
  quoted
  quoting
quotient

R

rabbi
  pl rabbis
rabbit
rabble
rabid
rabies
raccoon, racoon
race
racecourse
racial
  adv racially
racialism
racialist
racism
racist
rack
racket, racquet
  a tennis racket
racket
  a noisy racket;
  an illegal racket
racketeer
raconteur
racoon *see*
  raccoon
racquet *see* racket
racy
radar
  a radar beam
radiance
radiant
radiate

radiated
radiating
radiation
radiator
radical
  adv radically.
radio
  pl **radios**
  radioed
  radioing
radioactive
radiologist
radiology
radiotherapist
radiotherapy
radish
  pl radishes
radium
radius
  pl radii
raffia
raffle
raffled
raffling
raft
rafter
rag
  ragged
  They ragged
  the new boy
  ragging
ragamuffin
rage
  raged
  He raged and swore
  raging
ragged [ragd] *see*
  rag
ragged ['ragid]

ragged clothes
raid
raider

*The police caught
the raider*

rail
railing
railway
raiment
rain

*wind and rain:
to rain heavily*

rained
raining
rainbow
rainy
raise

*to raise a family:
to raise one's arm*

raised
raising
raisin
rajah
rake
raked
raking
rakish
rally

pl **rallies**

rallied
rallying
ram
rammed
ramming
ramble
rambled
rambling
rambler
ramification

ramp
rampage
rampaged
rampaging
rampant

*the lion rampant:
Violence is rampant*

rampart

*the rampart round
the castle*

ran *see* run
ranch

pl **ranches**

rancid
rancorous
rancour
rand
random
rang *see* ring
range
ranged
ranging
ranger
rank
rankle
rankled
rankling
ransack
ransom
ransomed
ransoming
rant
rap
rapped

He rapped on the door

rapping
rapacious
rape
raped

*He raped and
murdered her*

raping
rapid
rapidity
rapier
rapped *see* rap
rapt

*gazing with rapt
attention*

rapture
rapturous
rare
rarefied
rarely
raring
rarity

pl **rarities**

rascal

adv **rascally**

rash
rasher
rasp
raspberry

pl **raspberries**

rat
ratted

*The dog ratted: His
friends ratted on him*

ratting
ratchet
rate
rated

*They rated him
the best pilot*

rating
rateable
rather
ratification

ratify
  ratified
  ratifying
rating
ratio
  pl ratios
ration
  rationed
  rationing
rational
  adv **rationally**
rationalization,
  -isation
rationalize, -ise
  rationalized
  rationalizing
ratted *see* rat
rattle
  rattled
  rattling
rattlesnake
ratty
raucous
ravage
  ravaged
  ravaging
rave
  raved
  raving
raven
ravenous
ravine
ravishing
ray
  pl rays
rayon
raze
  to raze a city
  to the ground

razed
razing
razor
reach
react
reaction
reactionary
read [rēd]
  to read a book
read [red]
  He read that book
reading
reader
readily
readiness
ready
real
  a real diamond:
  a real friend
realism
realist
realistic
  adv realistically
reality
  pl realities
realization,
  -isation
realize, -ise
  realized
  realizing
really
realm
ream
reap
  reaped
  reaping
reaper
rear
  reared

rearing
rearguard
reason
  reasoned
  reasoning
reasonable
  adv reasonably
reassurance
reassure
  reassured
  reassuring
rebate
rebel
  rebelled
  rebelling
rebellion
rebellious
rebound
rebuff
rebuke
  rebuked
  rebuking
rebut
  rebutted
  rebutting
rebuttal
recalcitrance
recalcitrant
recall
  recalled
  recalling
recant
recap
  recapped
  recapping
recapitulate
  recapitulated
  recapitulating
recapitulation

recapture
  recaptured
  recapturing
recede
  receded
  receding
receipt
receive
  received
  receiving
receiver
recent
recently
receptacle
reception
receptionist
receptive
recess
  pl recesses
recession
recipe
recipient
reciprocal
  adv reciprocally
reciprocate
  reciprocated
  reciprocating
recital
recitation
recite
  recited
  reciting
reckless
reckon
  reckoned
  reckoning
reclaim
reclamation
recline
170

reclined
reclining
recluse
recognition
recognizable,
  -isable
  adv recognizably
recognize, -ise
  recognized
  recognizing
recoil
  recoiled
  recoiling
recollect
recollection
recommend
recommendation
recompense
reconcile
  reconciled
  reconciling
reconciliation
recondite
reconnaissance
reconnoitre
  reconnoitred
  reconnoitring
record
recorder
recording
recount
recoup
  recouped
  recouping
recourse
recover
  recovered
  recovering
recovery

re-creation
  a skilful re-creation
  of the Victorian
  atmosphere in the film
recreation
  She swims for
  recreation
recrimination
recruit
  recruited
  recruiting
recruitment
rectangle
rectangular
rectify
  rectified
  rectifying
rectitude
rector
rectory
  pl rectories
rectum
recumbent
recuperate
  recuperated
  recuperating
recuperation
recuperative
recur
  recurred
  recurring
recurrence
recurrent
red
  a red dress
redden
  reddened
  reddening
redeem

Redeemer
redeeming
redemption
redeploy
  redeployed
  redeploying
red-handed
redness
redolent
redouble
  redoubled
  redoubling
redoubtable
redress
reduce
  reduced
  reducing
reduction
redundancy
  pl redundancies
redundant
reed
  a broken reed: a reed
  by the pond: a reed of
  a musical instrument

reedy
reef
reefer
reek
reel
  a Scottish reel:
  to reel drunkenly

  reeled
  reeling
refectory
  pl refectories
refer
  referred
  referring

referee
reference
referendum
  pl referenda,
    referendums
refine
  refined
  refining
refinement
refinery
  pl refineries
reflect
reflection
reflective
  adv reflectively
reflector
reflex
reflexive
reform
reformation
reformer
refraction
refractory
refrain
  refrained
  refraining
refresh
refresher course
refreshment
refrigerator
refuel
  refuelled
  refuelling
refuge
  to find refuge
  from danger
refugee
  He is a war refugee
refund

refusal
refuse [rə'fūz]
  Did you refuse to go?
  refused
  refusing
refuse ['refūs]
  kitchen refuse
refute
  refuted
  refuting
regain
  regained
  regaining
regal
  a stately and regal
  carriage

  adv regally
regale
  to regale him with
  humorous stories

  regaled
  regaling
regalia
regard
regarding
regardless
regatta
  pl regattas
regency
regeneration
regent
regicide
régime
regiment
regimental
regimentation
region
regional
  adv regionally

register
  registered
  registering
registrar
registry
  pl registries
regret
  regretted
  regretting
regretful
  adv regretfully
regrettable
  adv regrettably
regular
regularity
regulate
  regulated
  regulating
regulation
regulator
regurgitate
  regurgitated
  regurgitating
rehabilitate
  rehabilitated
  rehabilitating
rehabilitation
rehearsal
rehearse
  rehearsed
  rehearsing
reign
  How long did
  Victoria reign?
  reigned
  reigning
reimburse
  reimbursed
  reimbursing

rein
  the reins of a horse:
  to rein in the horse
  reined
  reining
reincarnation
reindeer
  pl reindeer
reinforce
  reinforced
  reinforcing
reinforcements
reinstate
  reinstated
  reinstating
reinstatement
reiterate
  reiterated
  reiterating
reiteration
reiterative
reject
rejection
rejoice
  rejoiced
  rejoicing
rejoinder
rejuvenate
  rejuvenated
  rejuvenating
relapse
  relapsed
  relapsing
relate
  related
  relating
relation
relationship
relative

adv relatively
relax
relaxation
relay
  relayed
  relaying
release
  released
  releasing
relegate
  relegated
  relegating
relegation
relent
relentless
relevance
relevant
reliable
  adv reliably
reliance
reliant
relic
relief
  a sigh of relief
relieve
  to relieve her pain
  relieved
  relieving
religion
religious
relinquish
relish
  pl relishes
reluctance
reluctant
rely
  relied
  relying
remain

remained
remaining
remainder
remand
remark
remarkable
  adv remarkably
remedy
  pl remedies
remedied
remedying
remember
remembered
remembering
remembrance
remind
reminder
reminisce
reminisced
reminiscing
reminiscence
reminiscent
remiss
remission
remit
  remitted
  remitting
remittance
remnant
remonstrance
remonstrate
  remonstrated
  remonstrating
remorse
remorseful
  adv remorsefully
remorseless
remote
  adv remotely

removal
remove
  removed
  removing
remunerate
  remunerated
  remunerating
remuneration
remunerative
renal
render
  rendered
  rendering
rendezvous
  pl rendezvous
renegade
renew
renewal
rennet
renounce
  renounced
  renouncing
renovate
  renovated
  renovating
renovation
renown
  renowned
rent
rental
renunciation
reorganization,
  -isation
reorganize, -ise
  reorganized
  reorganizing
rep
repaid *see* repay
repair

repaired
repairing
reparation
repartee
repast
repatriate
  repatriated
  repatriating
repatriation
repay
  repaid
  repaying
  repayment
repeal
  repealed
  repealing
repeat
  repeated
  repeating
  repeatedly
repel
  repelled
  repelling
repellent,
  repellant
repent
repentance
repentant
repercussion
repertoire
repertory
repetition
repetitious
repetitive
  adv repetitively
replace
  replaced
  replacing
replacement

173

replenish
replete
replica
 pl replicas
reply
 pl replies
replied
replying
report
reporter
repose
repository
 pl repositories
reprehensible
 adv reprehensibly
represent
representation
representative
repress
repression
repressive
reprieve
 reprieved
 reprieving
reprimand
reprisal
reproach
 pl reproaches
reproachful
 adv reproachfully
reprobate
reproduce
 reproduced
 reproducing
reproduction
reproof
 a look of reproof
reprove
 to reprove the

naughty child
reproved
reproving
reptile
reptilian
republic
republican
repudiate
 repudiated
 repudiating
 repudiation
repugnance
repugnant
repulsive
 adv repulsively
reputable
reputation
repute
reputed
reputedly
request
requiem
require
 required
 requiring
 requirement
requisite
rescind
rescue
 rescued
rescuing
research
 pl researches
researcher
resemblance
resemble
 resembled
 resembling
resent

resentful
 adv resentfully
resentment
reservation
reserve
 reserved
 reserving
 reserved
reservoir
reside
 resided
 residing
residence
resident
residential
residual
residue
resign
 resigned
 resigning
resignation
resilience
resilient
resin
resinous
resist
resistance
resolute
 adv resolutely
resolution
resolve
 resolved
 resolving
resonance
resonant
resonate
 resonated
 resonating
resort

resounding
resource
resourceful
respect
respectability
respectable
 adv respectably
respectful
 a respectful salute
 adv respectfully
respective
 *They went to their
 respective homes*
 adv respectively
respiration
respirator
respite
resplendent
respond
response
responsibility
 pl responsibilities
responsible
 adv responsibly
responsive
rest
 *take a rest:
 rest in peace*
restaurant
restaurateur
restful
 adv restfully
restitution
restive
 adv restively
restless
restoration
restore
 restored

restoring
restrain
 restrained
 restraining
 restraint
restrict
 restriction
 restrictive
result
 resultant
resume
 resumed
 resuming
résumé
 resumption
resurgence
resurgent
resurrect
resurrection
resuscitate
 resuscitated
 resuscitating
 resuscitation
retail
 retailed
 retailing
retailer
retain
 retained
 retaining
 retainer
retaliate
 retaliated
 retaliating
 retaliation
retarded
retch
 *The sight of blood
 makes him retch*

retention
retentive
reticence
reticent
retina
 pl retinas, retinae
retinue
retiral
retire
 retired
 retiring
 retirement
retort
retrace
 retraced
 retracing
retract
 retractable
 retraction
retreat
 retreated
 retreating
retribution
retrieve
 retrieved
 retrieving
 retriever
retrograde
retrospect
retrospective
 adv
 retrospectively
return
returnable
reunion
reunite
 reunited
 reuniting
reveal

revealed
revealing
reveille
revel
revelled
revelling
revelation
reveller
revelry
revenge
revenged
revenging
revenue
reverberate
reverberated
reverberating
reverberation
revere
revered
revering
reverence
Reverend
reverent
reverential
adv reverentially
reverie
reversal
reverse
reversed
reversing
reversible
reversion
revert
review
*the review of his
new play: to review
a novel*
reviewer
revile

reviled
reviling
revise
revised
revising
revision
revival
revive
revived
reviving
revoke
revoked
revoking
revolt
revolting
revolution
revolutionary
pl revolutionaries
revolutionize, -ise
revolutionized
revolutionizing
revolve
revolved
revolving
revolver
revue
a musical revue
revulsion
reward
rhapsodize, -ise
rhapsodized
rhapsodizing
rhapsody
pl rhapsodies
rhetoric
rhetorical
adv rhetorically
rheumatic
rheumatism

rhinoceros
pl rhinoceroses
rhododendron
rhubarb
rhyme
*Cat is a rhyme
for rat: Do these
words rhyme?*

rhymed
rhyming
rhythm
rhythmic,
rhythmical
adv rhythmically
rib
ribald
ribbed
ribbon
rice
rich
riches
richness
rickets
rickety
rickshaw
ricochet
ricocheted
ricocheting
rid
rid
ridding
riddance
ridden *see* ride
riddle
riddled
riddling
ride
rode
He rode on a horse

ridden
*He has ridden
on a horse*

riding

rider

ridge

ridicule

ridiculed

ridiculing

ridiculous

rife

riff-raff

rifle

rifled

rifling

rift

rig

rigged

rigging

right

*the road on the right:
the right answer:
the right to vote*

righteous

righteousness

rightful

adv rightfully

rigid

rigmarole

rigorous

rigour

rim

rime

the rime on the grass

rind

ring

*an engagement ring:
to ring a racing
pigeon*

ringed

He ringed the pigeons

ringing

ring

to ring the bells

rang

The bell rang

rung

I have rung the bell

ringing

ringed *see* ring

rink

rinse

rinsed

rinsing

riot

rioted

rioting

rioter

riotous

rip

ripped

ripping

ripe

ripen

ripened

ripening

ripeness

ripple

rippled

rippling

rise

rose

The sun rose

risen

The sun has risen

rising

risk

risky

risotto

rissole

rite

*to perform a
religious rite*

ritual

adv **ritually**

rivet

riveted

riveting

rivulet

road

a main road

roam

roamed

roaming

roar

roared

roaring

roast

rob

robbed

robbing

robbery

pl robberies

robe

robin

robot

robust

rock

rocker

rockery

pl rockeries

rocket

rocketed

rocketing

rocky

rode *see* ride

rodent

roe
a roe deer: cod roe

rogue

roguish

rôle
the rôle of Hamlet

roll
*a roll of carpet:
to roll a ball*

roller

rollicking

Roman

romance

romantic
adv romantically

romp

roof
pl roofs

rook

rookery
pl rookeries

roomy

root
rooted
rooting

rope
roped
roping

ropy

rosary
pl rosaries

rose *see* rise

rose

rosemary

rosette

roster

rostrum
pl rostrums,
rostra

178

rosy

rot
rotted
rotting

rota
pl rotas

rotary

rotate
rotated
rotating

rotation

rote
*He learnt the answers
by rote*

rotten

rotter

rotund

rouge

rough
*a rough surface:
a rough sea*

roughage

roughen
roughened
roughening

roulette

round

rounders

rouse
roused
rousing

rout
*the rout of
Napoleon's army*

route
*the quickest route
to Edinburgh*

routine
adv routinely

rove
roved
roving

rover

row [rō]
*a row of cabbages:
to row a boat*

rowed
He rowed the boat

rowing

row [row]
a noisy row

rowan

rowdy

rowdyism

rowed *see* row

rower

rowing boat

rowlock

royal
adv royally

royalist

royalty
pl royalties

rub
rubbed
rubbing

rubber

rubbish

rubble

ruby
pl rubies

rucksack

rudder

ruddy

rude
adv rudely

rudeness

rudimentary

rudiments
rue
  rued
  ruing
rueful
  adv ruefully
ruff
  a ruff round the neck
ruffian
ruffle
  ruffled
  ruffling
rug
Rugby
rugged
ruin
  ruined
  ruining
ruination
ruinous
ruinously
rule
  ruled
  ruling
ruler
rum
rumble
  rumbled
  rumbling
ruminant
ruminate
  ruminated
  ruminating
rummage
  rummaged
  rummaging
rumour
rump
rumple

rumpled
rumpling
rumpus
run
  ran
  He ran away
  run
  He has run away
  running
rune
rung *see* ring
  rung
  the rung of the ladder
runner
runner-up
  pl runners-up
runway
rupee
rupture
  ruptured
  rupturing
rural
ruse
rush
  pl rushes
rusk
russet
rust
rustic
rustle
  rustled
  rustling
rustler
rusty
rut
  rutted
  rutting
ruthless
ruthlessness

rye
  rye bread

S

Sabbath
sable
sabotage
sabre
saccharine
sachet
sack
sacrament
sacred
sacrifice
  sacrificed
  sacrificing
sacrificial
sacrilege
sacrilegious
sacrosanct
sad
  compar sadder
  superl saddest
  adv sadly
sadden
  saddened
  saddening
saddle
  saddled
  saddling
saddler
sadism
sadist
sadistic
  adv sadistically
sadness
safari
safe

179

adv safely
safeguard
safety
saffron
sag
  sagged
  sagging
saga
  pl sagas
sagacious
sagacity
sage
  adv sagely
sago
said *see* say
sail
  a sail round the
  bay: to sail a boat
  sailed
  sailing
sailor
saint
saintly
sake
salaam
salad
salami
salary
  pl salaries
sale
  a furniture sale
salesman
salient
saline
saliva
salivary
salivate
  salivated
  salivating

sallow
sally
  pl sallies
  sallied
  sallying
salmon
salon
  a hairdressing salon
saloon
  a saloon car:
  a saloon bar
salt
salty
salubrious
salutary
salutation
salute
  saluted
  saluting
salvage
  salvaged
  salvaging
salvation
salve
  salved
  salving
salver
salvo
  pl salvos, salvoes
same
sameness
sample
  sampled
  sampling
sampler
sanatorium
  pl sanatoriums,
  sanatoria
sanctify

sanctified
sanctifying
sanctimonious
sanction
sanctioned
sanctioning
sanctity
sanctuary
  pl sanctuaries
sand
sandal
sandpaper
sandwich
  pl sandwiches
sandy
sane
  adv sanely
saneness
sang *see* sing
sanguine
  adv sanguinely
sanitary
sanitation
sanity
sank *see* sink
sap
  sapped
  sapping
sapling
sapphire
sarcasm
sarcastic
  adv sarcastically
sarcophagus
  pl sarcophagi,
  sarcophaguses
sardine
sardonic
  adv sardonically

sari
sarong
sartorial
sash
  pl sashes
sat *see* sit
Satan
satanic
satchel
sated
satellite
satiate
  satiated
  satiating
satiety
satin
satire
satirical
  adv satirically
satirist
satisfaction
satisfactory
  adv satisfactorily
satisfy
  satisfied
  satisfying
saturate
  saturated
  saturating
saturation
Saturday
saturnine
satyr
sauce
saucepan
saucer
saucy
  adv saucily
sauerkraut

saunter
  sauntered
  sauntering
sausage
savage
  adv savagely
savagery
save
  saved
  saving
  savings
saviour
  Christ the Saviour
savour
  *to savour the
  delicious wine*
savoury
  pl savouries
saw *see* see
saw
  sawed
  *He sawed the tree
  down*
  sawn
  *He has sawn off
  the branch*
  sawing
saxophone
say
  said
  saying
scab
scabbard
scabby
scabies
scaffold
scaffolding
scald
scale

scallop
scalloped
scallywag
scalp
scalpel
scaly
scamp
scamper
  scampered
  scampering
scampi
scan
  scanned
  scanning
scandal
scandalize, -ise
  scandalized
  scandalizing
scandalmonger
scandalous
scansion
scant
scanty
  adv scantily
scapegoat
scar
  scarred
  His cheek is scarred
  scarring
scarce
scarcely
scarcity
  pl scarcities
scare
  scared
  *She was scared of
  the dark*
  scaring
scarf

pl scarves, scarfs
scarlet
scarred *see* scar
scathing
scatter
  scattered
  scattering
scavenger
scene
  *the first scene of
  the play: the scene
  of the crime*

scenery
scenic
scent
  *the scent of spring
  flowers*
sceptic
  *A sceptic doesn't
  believe anyone*

sceptical
  adv sceptically
scepticism
sceptre
schedule
scheme
  schemed
  scheming
schism
schizophrenia
schizophrenic
scholar
scholarly
scholarship
scholastic
  adv scholastically
school
  schooled
  schooling

schoolfellow
schooner
sciatica
science
scientific
  adv scientifically
scientist
scintillate
  scintillated
  scintillating
scissors
scoff
scold
  scolding
scone
scoop
  scooped
  scooping
scooter
scope
scorch
score
  scored
  scoring
scorer
scorn
scornful
  adv scornfully
scorpion
scoundrel
scour
  scoured
  scouring
scourge
  scourged
  scourging
scout
scowl
scrabble

scrabbled
scrabbling
scraggy
scramble
  scrambled
  scrambling
scrap
  scrapped
  *They have scrapped
  the plans*
  scrapping
scrape
  scraped
  *She scraped her arm
  on the stone wall*
  scraping
scrapped *see*
  scrap
scratch
  pl scratches
scrawl
scrawny
scream
  screamed
  screaming
scree
screech
  pl screeches
screed
screen
screw
  screwed
  screwing
scribble
  scribbled
  scribbling
scripture
scroll
scrub

scrubbed
scrubbing
scruff
  adv scruffily
scruffy
scruple
scrupulous
  adv scrupulously
scrutinize, -ise
  scrutinized
  scrutinizing
scrutiny
scuffle
scullery
  pl sculleries
sculptor
  *He is an artist
  and a sculptor*
sculpture
  *a beautiful piece
  of sculpture*
scum
scupper
  scuppered
  scuppering
scurrilous
scurry
  scurried
  scurrying
scurvy
scuttle
  scuttled
  scuttling
scythe
sea
  ships on the sea
seagull
seal
  sealed

sealing
  *the sealing of the
  envelope: sealing wax*
seam
  *to sew a seam:
  a coal seam*
seamy
séance
sear
  to sear meat
  seared
  searing
search
  pl searches
season
  seasoned
  seasoning
seasonable
seasonal
  adv seasonally
seat
  seated
  seating
seaweed
secateurs
secede
  seceded
  seceding
secession
secluded
seclusion
second
secondary
second-hand
secrecy
secret
  *They kept their
  marriage a secret:
  a secret plan*

secretarial
secretary
  pl secretaries
secrete
  *to secrete a dagger
  under a cloak*
  secreted
  secreting
secretion
secretive
  adv secretively
sect
sectarian
section
sector
secular
secure
  adv securely
  secured
  securing
security
  pl securities
sedate
  adv sedately
sedation
sedative
sedentary
sediment
sedition
seditious
seduce
  seduced
  seducing
seduction
seductive
  adv seductively
see
  *Did you see him?:
  to see clearly*

saw
I saw you
seen
I have seen him
seeing
seed
seedling
seedy
seek
sought
seeking
seem
They seem friendly
seemed
seeming
seemingly
seemly
seen *see* see
seep
seeped
seeping
seer
The seer foretold her death
seesaw
seethe
seethed
seething
segment
segregate
segregated
segregating
segregation
seismic
seize
seized
seizing
seizure
seldom

select
selection
selective
self
pl selves
selfish
sell
to sell flowers from a stall
sold
selling
Sellotape ®
selvage
semblance
seminar
semolina
senate
senator
send
sent
I sent a letter
sending
senile
senility
senior
seniority
sensation
sensational
adv sensationally
sense
sensed
sensing
senseless
sensible
adv sensibly
sensitive
adv sensitively
sensitivity
sensory

sensual
a sensual face
adv sensually
sensuous
the sensuous quality of the sculpture
sent *see* send
sentence
sentenced
sentencing
sentimental
adv sentimentally
sentimentality
sentinel
separate
adv separately
separated
separating
separation
September
septic
a septic wound: a septic tank
septuagenarian
sepulchral
sepulchre
sequel
sequence
sequestered
sequin
seraph
pl seraphs, seraphim
seraphic
sere
withered and sere
serenade
serene
adv serenely

serenity
serf
serge
sergeant
serial
  a television serial:
  a magazine serial
series
  a series of plays
  pl series
serious
  in a serious mood
sermon
serpent
serrated
serried
serum
servant
serve
  served
  serving
service
serviceable
serviette
servile
  adv servilely
servility
session
set
  set
  setting
settee
setter
settle
  settled
  settling
settlement
settler
seven

seventeen
seventeenth
seventh
seventieth
seventy
sever
  severed
  severing
several
severance
severe
  adv severely
severity
sew
  to sew a seam
  sewed
  She sewed the seam
  sewn
  She has sewn it
  sewing
sewage
sewed *see* sew
sewer ['sūər]
sewer ['sōər]
  a sewer and a knitter
sewn *see* sew
sex
sexagenarian
sextant
  a ship's sextant
sexton
  The sexton tolled
  the bell
sexual
  adv sexually
shabby
  adv shabbily
shackles
shade

shaded
shading
shadow
shady
shaft
shaggy
shake
  shook
  She shook the child
  shaken
  She has shaken
  the child
  shaking
shaky
  adv shakily
shall
  should
shallot
shallow
sham
  shammed
  shamming
shambles
shame
  shamed
  shaming
shameful
  adv shamefully
shameless
shammy *see*
  chamois
shampoo
  shampooed
  shampooing
shamrock
shape
  shaped
  shaping
shapeless

185

shapely
share
  shared
  sharing
sharp
sharpen
  sharpened
  sharpening
sharpener
shatter
  shattered
  shattering
shave
  shaved
  shaving
shawl
sheaf
  pl **sheaves**
shear
  to shear sheep
  sheared
  He sheared the sheep
  shorn
  He has shorn the sheep
  shearing
shears
sheath
shed
sheep
sheepish
sheer
  a sheer drop:
  sheer delight
  sheered
  The car sheered off
  the road
  sheering
sheet
186

sheikh
shekel
shelf
  a wooden shelf
  pl **shelves**
shell
shelter
  sheltered
  sheltering
shelve
  to shelve the problem:
  The cliff shelves
  slightly
shepherd
sherbet
sheriff
sherry
shied *see* shy
shield
shier, shiest *see*
  shy
shift
shiftless
shifty
  adv **shiftily**
shilling
shimmer
  shimmered
  shimmering
shin
shine
  shone
  shining
shingles
shiny
ship
  shipped
  shipping
shipwreck

shire
shirk
shirker
shirt
shiver
  shivered
  shivering
shoal
shock
  shocking
shod *see* shoe
shoddy
  adv **shoddily**
shoe
  to shoe a horse
  shod
  shoeing
shone *see* shine
shoo
  to shoo the birds away
  shooed
  shooing
shook *see* shake
shoot
  to shoot dead
  shot
  shooting
shop
  shopped
  shopping
shopper
shore
shorn *see* shear
short
shortage
shortcoming
shorten
  shortened
  shortening

shorthand

shortly

shot *see* shoot

should *see* shall

shoulder

  shouldered

  shouldering

shout

shove

  shoved

  shoving

shovel

  shovelled

  shovelling

show

  showed

  He showed me the book

  shown

  He has shown me the book

  showing

shower

  showered

  showering

showery

shown *see* show

showy

  adv showily

shrank *see* shrink

shrapnel

shred

  shredded

  shredding

shrew

shrewd

shrewish

shriek

  shrieked

shrieking

shrill

  adv **shrilly**

shrimp

shrine

shrink

  shrank

  That dress shrank

  shrunk

  That dress has shrunk

  shrinking

shrivel

  shrivelled

  shrivelling

shroud

shrub

shrubbery

  pl shrubberies

shrug

  shrugged

  shrugging

shrunk *see* shrink

shrunken

shudder

  shuddered

  shuddering

shuffle

  shuffled

  shuffling

shun

  shunned

  shunning

shunt

shut

  shut

  shutting

shutter

shuttle

shy

compar shyer, shier

superl shyest, shiest

adv shyly

shy

  shied

  shying

shyness

sibilant

Sibyl

sick

sicken

  sickened

  sickening

sickle

sickly

side

  sided

  siding

sideboard

sideways

siding

sidle

  sidled

  sidling

siege

siesta

sieve

  sieved

  sieving

sift

sigh

  sighed

  sighing

sight

  What a sight he is in that hat! : The sight of him made her

*cry: to sight land
from the ship*

sighted
sighting
sightseeing
sign
  signed
  signing
signal
  signalled
  signalling
signatory
  pl signatories
signature
signet
  a signet ring
significance
significant
signify
  signified
  signifying
silage
silence
  silenced
  silencing
silencer
silent
silhouette
  silhouetted
  silhouetting
silicon
  *Silicon is a common
  element*
silicone
  silicone polish
silk
silky
sill
silly
188

silo
  pl silos
silt
silver
silvery
similar
similarity
  pl similarities
simile
simmer
  simmered
  simmering
simper
  simpered
  simpering
simple
  adv **simply**
simpleton
simplicity
simplification
simplify
  simplified
  simplifying
simply
simulate
  simulated
  simulating
simulation
simultaneous
sin
  sinned
  sinning
since
sincere
  adv **sincerely**
sincerity
sinecure
sinew
sinful

adv sinfully
sing
  sang
  He sang a song
  sung
  He has sung a song
  singing
  singing a song
singe
  singed
  singeing
  *singeing the shirt
  with the iron*
single
  adv singly
  singled
  singling
singleness
singlet
singular
singularity
sinister
sink
  sank
  The ship sank
  sunk
  The ship has sunk
  sinking
sinner
sinuous
  sinuous curves
sinus
  He has sinus trouble
  pl sinuses
sip
  sipped
  sipping
siphon
  siphoned

siphoning
sir
sire
siren
sirloin
sisal
sister
sister-in-law
  pl sisters-in-law
sisterly
sit
  sat
  sitting
site
  the site of the
  new factory
  sited
  siting
sit-in
sitting-room
situated
situation
six
sixteen
sixteenth
sixth
sixtieth
sixty
size
  sized
  sizing
sizeable, sizable
sizzle
  sizzled
  sizzling
skate
  skated
  skating
skein

skeletal
skeleton
sketch
  pl sketches
sketchy
  adv sketchily
skew
skewer
  skewered
  skewering
ski
  pl skis
  He fastened on
  his skis
  skied
  skiing
skid
  skidded
  skidding
skiff
skilful
  adv skilfully
skill
skilled
skim
  skimmed
  skimming
skimp
skimpy
  adv skimpily
skin
  skinned
  skinning
skinny
skip
  skipped
  skipping
skipper
skirmish

pl skirmishes
skirt
skirting
skittish
skittle
skulk
skull
skunk
sky
  pl skies
  blue skies
skylark
skylight
slack
slacken
  slackened
  slackening
slag
slain see slay
slake
  slaked
  slaking
slalom
slam
  slammed
  slamming
slander
  slandered
  slandering
slanderous
slang
slant
slap
  slapped
  slapping
slapdash
slash
  pl slashes
slat

189

slate
slated
The roof is slated:
His book was slated
by the critics
slating
slatted
a slatted wooden fence
slaughter
slaughtered
slaughtering
slave
slaver
slavered
slavering
slavery
slavish
slay
to slay the enemy
slew
He slew his enemy
slain
He has slain the enemy
slaying
sledge
sledged
sledging
sleep
slept
sleeping
sleeper
sleepy
adv sleepily
sleet
sleeve
sleeveless
sleigh
a sleigh in the snow
sleight-of-hand

slender
slept *see* sleep
sleuth
slew *see* slay
slew
The car began to
slew round
slewed
slewing
slice
sliced
slicing
slick
slide
slid
sliding
slight
slightly
slightness
slim
slimmed
slimming
slimy
sling
slung
slinging
slink
slunk
slinking
slinky
adv slinkily
slip
slipped
slipping
slipper
slippery
slit
slit
slitting

slither
slithered
slithering
sliver
slobber
slobbered
slobbering
sloe
a ripe sloe
slog
slogged
slogging
slogan
slop
slopped
The water slopped
in the pail
slopping
slope
sloped
The hill sloped down
sloping
slopped *see* slop
sloppy
adv sloppily
slot
slotted
slotting
slothful
adv slothfully
slouch
slough [slow]
= a marsh
the slough of despond
slough [sluf]
to slough off skin
sloughed
sloughing
slovenly

190

slow
a slow train:
to slow down
sludge
slug
sluggish
sluice
slum
slumber
  slumbered
  slumbering
slump
slung *see* sling
slunk *see* slink
slur
  slurred
  slurring
slush
slushy
slut
sluttish
sly
  adv **slyly**
slyness
smack
small
smallness
smart
smash
  pl smashes
smattering
smear
  smeared
  smearing
smell
  smelled, smelt
  They smelled smoke:
  It smelt of fish
  smelling

smelly
smelt *see* smell
smelt
  to smelt ore
  smelted
  smelting
smile
  smiled
  smiling
smirk
smithereens
smithy
smitten
smock
  smocking
smog
smoke
  smoked
  smoking
  smokeless
  smoker
smoky
smooth
  smoothed
  smoothing
smother
  smothered
  smothering
smoulder
  smouldered
  smouldering
smudge
  smudged
  smudging
smug
smuggle
  smuggled
  smuggling
smuggler

smut
smutty
snack
snag
  snagged
  snagging
snail
snake
  snaked
  snaking
snap
  snapped
  snapping
snappy
  adv **snappily**
snare
  snared
  snaring
snarl
snatch
  pl snatches
sneak
sneaky
sneer
  sneered
  sneering
sneeze
  sneezed
  sneezing
sniff
snigger
  sniggered
  sniggering
snip
  snipped
  She snipped the thread
  snipping
snipe
  sniped

191

They sniped at the enemy

sniping

sniper

snipped *see* snip

snippet

snivel

snivelled

snivelling

snob

snobbery

snobbish

snooker

snoop

snooped

snooping

snooze

snoozed

snoozing

snore

snored

snoring

snorkel

snort

snout

snow

snowed

snowing

snowball

snowy

snub

snubbed

snubbing

snuff

snuffle

snuffled

snuffling

snug

snuggle

snuggled

snuggling

so

so beautiful: so much

soak

so-and-so

soap

soapiness

soapy

soar

to soar high in the air

soared

soaring

sob

sobbed

sobbing

sober

sobered

sobering

soberness

sobriety

soccer

sociability

sociable

He is friendly and sociable

adv sociably

sociableness

social

social history: a social occasion: social class

adv socially

socialism

socialist

socialistic

sociological

sociology

sock

socket

sod

soda

sodden

sofa

soft

soften

softened

softening

software

soggy

soil

soiled

soiling

sojourn

sojourned

sojourning

solace

solaced

solacing

solar

sold *see* sell

solder

to solder metal

soldered

soldering

soldier

The soldier left the army

soldiered

soldiering

sole

the sole of the foot: lemon sole: He is the sole survivor

adv solely

solemn

adv solemnly

solemnity
sol-fa
solicit
  solicited
  soliciting
solicitor
solicitous
solid
solidarity
solidify
  solidified
  solidifying
solidity
soliloquy
  pl soliloquies
solitary
solitude
solo
  pl solos
soloist
solstice
solubility
soluble
solution
solve
  solved
  solving
solvency
solvent
sombre
  adv sombrely
sombreness
sombrero
  pl sombreros
some
  some people
somebody
someone
somersault

something
somnolence
somnolent
son
  a son and daughter
son-in-law
  pl sons-in-law
sonata
song
songster
songstress
  pl songstresses
sonic
sonnet
sonorous
soon
sooner
soot
  soot in the chimney
soothe
  soothed
  soothing
sooty
sophisticated
sophistication
soporific
sopping
soprano
  pl sopranos
sorcerer
sorcery
sordid
sore
  a sore leg
  adv sorely
soreness
sorrel
sorrow
sorrowful

  adv sorrowfully
sorry
sort
sortie
SOS
sotto voce
soufflé
sought see seek
soul
  spirit and soul:
  the soul of kindness:
  a dear old soul:
  soul music
soulful
  adv soulfully
sound
soup
sour
source
souse
  soused
  sousing
southerly
  a southerly wind
southern
  the southern seas
sovereign
sovereignty
sow [sow]
  a sow in the pigsty
sow [sō]
  to sow seeds
  sowed
  He sowed seeds
  sown
  He has sown seeds
  sowing
sower
  a sower of seeds

193

soya bean
spa
space
  spaced
  spacing
spacecraft
spacious
spaciousness
spade
spaghetti
span
  spanned
  spanning
spangle
spaniel
spank
  spanking
spanner
spar
  sparred
    *He sparred with
    his opponent*
  sparring
spare
  spared
    They spared his life
  sparing
sparing
  adv **sparingly**
spark
sparkle
  sparkled
  sparkling
sparred *see* spar
sparrow
sparse
  adv sparsely
spartan
spasm

spasmodic
  adv
    spasmodically
spastic
spat *see* spit
spate
spatial
spats
spatter
  spattered
  spattering
spatula
spawn
speak
  spoke
    She spoke to me
  spoken
    He has spoken at last
  speaking
spear
special
  adv specially
specialist
speciality
  *Cream cakes are
  their speciality*
  pl specialities
specialization,
  -isation
specialize, -ise
  specialized
  specializing
specialty
  *Which medical
  specialty is he in?*
  pl specialties
species
  pl species
  animals of different

species
specific
  adv **specifically**
specification
specify
  specified
  specifying
specimen
specious
  a specious argument
speck
speckled
spectacle
spectacles
spectacular
  adv spectacularly
spectator
spectral
spectre
spectrum
  pl spectrums,
    spectra
speculate
  speculated
  speculating
speculation
speculative
  adv speculatively
sped *see* speed
speech
  pl speeches
speechless
speed
  speeded
    *The driver always
    speeded*
  sped
    *They sped along
    the path*

speeding
speedometer
speedy
  adv speedily
spell
  spelled, spelt
  spelling
spend
  spent
  spending
sperm
spew
sphagnum
sphere
spherical
sphinx
spice
spiciness
spick-and-span
spicy
spider
spidery
spiel
spike
spiked
spiky
spill
  spilled, spilt
  spilling
spillage
spin
  spun
  spinning
spinach
spinal
spindle
spindly
spin-drier
spine

spineless
spinet
spinner
spinney
  pl spinneys
spinster
spiral
  spiralled
  spiralling
spire
spirit
  spirited
  spiriting
spiritual
  adv spiritually
spiritualism
spiritualist
spit
  spat
  spitting
spite
spiteful
  adv spitefully
spittle
spittoon
splash
  pl splashes
splay
splay-footed
spleen
splendid
splendour
splice
  spliced
  splicing
splint
splinter
  splintered
  splintering

split
  split
  splitting
splutter
  spluttered
  spluttering
spoil
  spoilt, spoiled
  spoiling
spoke *see* speak
spoke
spoken *see* speak
spokesman
sponge
  sponged
  sponging
sponger
spongy
sponsor
  sponsored
  sponsoring
spontaneity
spontaneous
spoof
spooky
spool
spoon
  spooned
  spooning
spoonerism
spoonful
  pl spoonfuls
sporadic
  adv sporadically
sporran
sport
sporting
sportsman
  pl sportsmen

sportsmanlike
spot
  spotted
  spotting
spotless
spotlight
spotty
spouse
spout
  spouted
  spouting
sprain
  sprained
  spraining
sprang *see* spring
sprawl
spray
  sprayed
  spraying
spread
  spread
  spreading
spread-eagled
spree
sprig
sprightliness
sprightly
  adv sprightlily
spring
  sprang
  He sprang to his feet
  sprung
  He had sprung to his feet
  springing
sprinkle
  sprinkled
  sprinkling
sprinkler

sprint
sprinter
sprite
sprocket
sprout
  sprouted
  sprouting
spruce
  adv sprucely
sprung *see* spring
spry
  adv spryly
spun *see* spin
spur
  spurred
  spurring
spurious
spurn
spurt
sputter
  sputtered
  sputtering
sputum
spy
  pl spies
  spied
  spying
squabble
  squabbled
  squabbling
squad
squadron
squalid
squall
squally
squalor
squander
  squandered
  squandering

square
  adv squarely
squash
  to squash under foot:
  to squash the fruit
squash (rackets)
squat
  squatted
  squatting
squatter
squaw
squawk
  squawked
  squawking
squeak
  squeaked
  squeaking
squeaky
squeal
  squealed
  squealing
squeamish
squeeze
  squeezed
  squeezing
squelch
squib
squid
squiggle
squiggly
squint
squire
squirm
squirrel
squirt
stab
  stabbed
  stabbing
stability

196

stabilize, -ise
  stabilized
  stabilizing
  stabilizer, -iser
stable
staccato
stack
stadium
  pl stadiums
staff
  staffed
  staffing
stag
stage
  staged
  staging
stagger
  staggered
  staggering
stagnant
stagnate
  stagnated
  stagnating
stagnation
staid
  She is staid and
  respectable
stain
  stained
  staining
stainless
stair
  a winding stair
staircase
stake
  a wooden stake: a
  stake in the firm:
  to stake a claim
staked

staking
stalactite
stalagmite
stale
stalemate
stalk
  the stalk of the
  flower: to stalk off
  angrily: to stalk
  deer
stalker
stall
stallion
stalwart
stamen
stamina
stammer
  stammered
  stammering
stamp
stampede
  stampeded
  stampeding
stance
stanch, staunch
  to stanch the blood
stand
  stood
  standing
standard
standardization,
  -isation
standardize, -ise
  standardized
  standardizing
standby
stand-in
stand-offish
standstill

stank *see* stink
stanza
staple
star
  starred
  Who starred
  in that film?
  starring
starboard
starch
  pl starches
starchy
stardom
stare
  a disapproving stare:
  to stare in amazement
  stared
  She stared in
  amazement at him
  staring
stark
starling
starred *see* star
starry
start
startle
  startled
  startling
startling
starvation
starve
  starved
  starving
state
  stated
  stating
stately
statement
statesman

pl statesmen
statesmanlike
static
station
stationary
The car was stationary
stationer
stationery
pens, pencils and other stationery
statistical
adv **statistically**
statistician
statistics
statue
a statue of Nelson
statuesque
statuette
stature
status
status quo
statute
by statute of Parliament
statutory
staunch
a staunch supporter
staunch *see*
stanch
stave
staved, stove
staving
stay
stayed
We stayed at that hotel: She stayed unmarried
staying
steadfast
198

steadiness
steady
adv **steadily**
steadied
steadying
steak
steak and chips
steal
Did he steal the jewels?
stole
He stole the ring
stolen
He has stolen the ring
stealing
stealth
stealthy
adv **stealthily**
steam
steamed
steaming
steamer
steamy
steed
steel
iron and steel
steely
steep
steeped
steeping
steeple
steeplechase
steeplejack
steer
steered
steering
stem
stemmed
stemming

stench
stencil
stencilled
stencilling
stentorian
step
He climbed the wooden steps
stepped
stepping
stepmother
steppe
the steppes of Russia
stereo
stereophonic
stereotype
stereotyped
sterile
sterility
sterilization, -isation
sterilize, -ise
sterilized
sterilizing
sterling
stern
sternness
stertorous
stethoscope
stevedore
stew
steward
stewardess
pl **stewardesses**
stick
stuck
sticking
stickiness
stickler

sticky
stiff
stiffen
  stiffened
  stiffening
stifle
  stifled
  stifling
stigma
stile

  *Climb over the stile
  into the other field*

stiletto
  pl stilettos
still
stillborn
stillness
stilted
stilts
stimulant

  *Is that drug
  a stimulant?*

stimulate
  stimulated
  stimulating
stimulus

  *the stimulus provided
  by competing against
  others*
  pl stimuli

sting
  stung
  stinging
stingy
stink
  stank
  The pigsty stank
  stunk
  It has stunk for days

stinking
stint
stipend
stipulate
  stipulated
  stipulating
stipulation
stir
  stirred
  stirring
stirrup
stitch
  pl stitches
stoat
stock

  *He comes of noble
  stock: a stock of
  tinned food: stocks
  and shares: Criminals
  used to be put in the
  stocks: We do not
  stock newspapers*

stocked

  *He stocked many
  brands of whisky*

stocking
stockade
stockbroker
stocked *see* stock
stockiness
stocking
stocktaking
stocky
  adv stockily
  stockily-built
stodginess
stodgy
stoic
stoical

adv stoically
stoicism
stoke
  stoked
  He stoked the fire
  stoking
stoker
stole
stole *see* steal
stolen *see* steal
stolid
stolidity
stomach
stone
stony
  adv stonily
stood *see* stand
stooge
stool
stoop
  stooped
  stooping
stop
  stopped
  stopping
stoppage
stopper
storage
store
  stored
  storing
storey
  a four-storey building
  pl storeys
stork
storm
stormy
  adv stormily
story

199

a fairy story
pl **stories**
stout
stoutness
stove *see* stave
stove
stow
stowaway
straddle
  straddled
  straddling
straggle
  straggled
  straggling
straggly
straight
  a straight line:
  a straight actor
straighten
  straightened
  The dentist
  straightened her teeth
  straightening
straightness
strain
  strained
  straining
strainer
strait
  a strait between
  pieces of land
straitened
  in straitened
  circumstances
straitjacket
straitlaced
strand
strange
  adv **strangely**

strangeness
stranger
strangle
  strangled
  strangling
stranglehold
strangulation
strap
  strapped
  strapping
stratagem
strategic
  adv **strategically**
strategist
strategy
  pl **strategies**
stratification
stratified
stratosphere
stratum
  a stratum of rich ore:
  a stratum of society
  pl **strata**
stratus
  stratus clouds
straw
strawberry
  pl **strawberries**
stray
  strayed
  straying
streak
streakiness
streaky
stream
  streamed
  streaming
streamer
streamline

streamlined
streamlining
street
strength
strengthen
  strengthened
  strengthening
strenuous
stress
  pl **stresses**
  stressed
  stressing
stretch
  pl **stretches**
stretcher
strew
  strewed
  They strewed the
  flowers
  strewn
  strewn with
  wild flowers
  strewing
stricken
strict
stricture
stride
  strode
  striding
stridency
strident
strife
  quarrelling and strife
strike
  struck
  striking
string
  strung
  stringing

stringency
  pl stringencies
stringent
stringy
strip
  stripped
  He stripped the wood:
  They stripped the
  wallpaper off

  stripping
striped
  red and white striped
stripling
stripped *see* strip
stripy
strive
  to strive to do better
  strove
  He strove to do well
  striven
  He has striven
  striving
strode *see* stride
stroke
  stroked
  stroking
stroll
strong
stroppy
strove *see* strive
struck *see* strike
structural
  adv structurally
structure
structured
struggle
  struggled
  struggling
strum

strummed
strumming
strung *see* string
strut
  strutted
  strutting
strychnine
stub
  stubbed
  stubbing
stubble
stubborn
stubbornness
stubby
stucco
stuck *see* stick
stud
  studded
  studding
student
studio
  pl studios
studious
studiousness
study
  pl studies
  studied
  studying
stuff
  stuffing
stuffy
stultify
  stultified
  stultifying
stumble
  stumbled
  stumbling
stump
stumpy

stun
  stunned
  stunning
stung *see* sting
stunk *see* stink
stunt
  stunted
stupefaction
stupefy
  stupefied
  stupefying
stupendous
stupid
stupidity
stupor
sturdiness
sturdy
  adv sturdily
sturgeon
stutter
  stuttered
  stuttering
sty
  a pig in a sty
  pl sties
stye, sty
  a sty on the eye
  pl sties, styes
style
  style of dress:
  literary style
  styled
  styling
stylish
stylus
  pl styluses
suave
  adv suavely
suavity

201

subaltern
subcommittee
subconscious
subdue
  subdued
  subduing
subject
subjective
  adv subjectively
subjectiveness
subjectivity
subjugate
  subjugated
  subjugating
subjugation
sublieutenant
sublime
  adv sublimely
sublimity
submarine
submerge
  submerged
  submerging
submersion
submission
submissive
  adv submissively
submit
  submitted
  submitting
subordinate
  subordinated
  subordinating
suborn
  suborned
  suborning
subpoena
  subpoenaed
  subpoenaing

subscribe
  subscribed
  subscribing
subscription
subsequent
subservience
subservient
subside
  subsided
  subsiding
subsidence
subsidiary
  pl subsidiaries
subsidize, -ise
  subsidized
  subsidizing
subsidy
  pl subsidies
subsist
subsistence
subsoil
substance
substantial
  adv substantially
substantiate
  substantiated
  substantiating
substantive
substitute
  substituted
  substituting
substitution
subterfuge
subterranean
subtitle
subtle
  adv subtly
subtlety
  pl subtleties

subtract
subtraction
suburb
suburban
suburbia
subversive
  adv subversively
subway
succeed
  succeeded
  succeeding
success
  pl successes
successful
  adv successfully
succession
successive
  adv successively
successor
succinct
  adv succinctly
succour
  succoured
  succouring
succulence
succulent
succumb
  succumbed
  succumbing
such
suck
sucker
suckle
  suckled
  suckling
suction
sudden
suddenly
suddenness

suds
sue
 sued
 suing
 suede
  a suede jacket
suet
suffer
 suffered
 suffering
 sufferance
suffice
 sufficed
 sufficing
 sufficient
suffix
 pl suffixes
 suffocate
 suffocated
 suffocating
suffocation
suffrage
suffragette
suffuse
 suffused
 suffusing
suffusion
sugar
sugar-beet
sugared
sugary
suggest
suggestible
 suggestion
suggestive
 adv **suggestively**
suicidal
 suicide
suit [sōōt]

a suit of clothes:
This will suit you
 suited
 suiting
suitability
suitable
 adv **suitably**
suitcase
suite [swēt]
 a suite of rooms:
 a bedroom suite
suitor
sulk
sulky
 adv **sulkily**
sullen
 sullenness
sully
 sullied
 sullying
sulphur
sulphuric
sultan
sultana
sultry
 adv **sultrily**
sum
 a difficult sum
 summed
 summing
summarily
summarize, -ise
 summarized
 summarizing
summary
 a summary of our
 plans: a short
 summary
 of the plot of
 the play

 pl **summaries**
summer
summery
 a summery day:
 a summery dress
summit
summon
 summoned
 summoning
summons
 pl **summonses**
 sumptuous
sun
 The sun shone brightly
 sunned
 sunning
sunbathe
 sunbathed
 sunbathing
sunburn
sunburned,
 sunburnt
sundae
 an ice cream sundae
Sunday
 They went to church
 on Sunday
sundial
sundries
sundry
sung *see* sing
sunk *see* sink
sunken
 sunken cheeks
sunny
 adv **sunnily**
suntan
 suntanned
 suntanning

sup
  supped
  supping
super
  a super holiday
superannuated
superannuation
superb
supercilious
superficial
  adv superficially
superfluity
superfluous
superhuman
superintend
superintendence
superintendent
superior
superiority
superlative
  adv superlatively
supermarket
supernatural
  adv
    supernaturally
supersede
  superseded
  superseding
supersonic
superstition
superstitious
  adv
    superstitiously
supervise
  supervised
  supervising
supervision
supervisor
supine

supper
  *They had supper
  at 9 pm*
supplant
supple
  adv supply
supplement
supplementary
suppleness
suppliant
supplication
supply
  pl supplies
  supplied
  supplying
support
supporter
suppose
  supposed
  supposing
supposedly
supposition
suppress
suppression
suppurate
  suppurated
  suppurating
supremacy
supreme
  adv supremely
surcharge
sure
surely
surety
  pl sureties
surf
surface
  surfaced
  surfacing

surfeit
surfing
surge
  surged
  surging
surgeon
surgery
  pl surgeries
surgical
  adv surgically
surliness
surly
  adv surlily
surmise
  surmised
  surmising
surmountable
surname
surpass
surplice
  a priest's surplice
surplus
  a surplus of butter
surprise
  surprised
  surprising
surrender
  surrendered
  surrendering
surreptitious
surround
surroundings
surtax
surveillance
survey
  surveyed
  surveying
surveyor
survival

survive
survived
surviving
survivor
susceptibility
susceptible
suspect
suspend
suspender
suspense
suspension
suspicion
suspicious
sustain
sustained
sustaining
sustenance
swab
swabbed
swabbing
swaddle
swaddled
swaddling
swagger
swaggered
swaggering
swain
swallow
swam *see* swim
swamp
swan
swank
swanky
swap, swop
swapped,
swopped
swapping,
swopping
swarm

swarthy
swashbuckling
swat
swatted
swatting
swathed
sway
swayed
swaying
swear
swore
He swore to be true
sworn
*He has sworn
to be true*
swearing
sweat
sweated
sweating
sweater
sweaty
swede
*The farmer grows
swedes*
Swedish
sweep
swept
sweeping
sweet
*a sweet smile:
a sweet orange:
to suck a sweet*
sweeten
sweetened
sweetening
sweetener
sweetheart
sweetness
swell

swelled
His leg swelled
swollen
His leg has swollen
swelling
swelter
sweltered
sweltering
swept *see* sweep
swerve
swerved
swerving
swift
swiftness
swig
swigged
swigging
swill
swim
swam
She swam a length
swum
She has swum a length
swimming
swimmer
swimmingly
swindle
swindled
swindling
swindler
swine
swing
swung
swinging
swinging on a gate
swingeing
swingeing cuts
swinish
swipe

swiped
swiping
swirl
swish
switch
  pl switches
switchboard
swivel
  swivelled
  swivelling
swollen *see* swell
swoop
  swooped
  swooping
swop *see* swap
sword
swordfish
swore, sworn *see*
  swear
swum *see* swim
swung *see* swing
sycamore
sycophant
syllabic
syllable
syllabus
  pl syllabuses,
    syllabi
sylph
symbol
  a mathematical
  symbol:
  a symbol of the
  king's authority
symbolic
  adv symbolically
symbolism
symbolize, -ise

symbolized
symbolizing
symmetrical
  adv
    symmetrically
symmetry
sympathetic
  adv
    sympathetically
sympathize, -ise
sympathized
sympathizing
sympathy
symphony
  pl symphonies
symposium
  pl symposia,
    symposiums
symptom
symptomatic
synagogue
synchronize, -ise
synchronized
synchronizing
syncopate
syncopated
syncopating
syncopation
syndicate
synod
synonym
synonymous
synopsis
  pl synopses
syntax
synthesis
synthesize, -ise
synthesized
synthesizing

synthetic
  adv synthetically
syringe
syrup
syrupy
system
systematic
  adv
    systematically

T

tab
tabard
tabby
  pl tabbies
tabernacle
table
  tabled
  tabling
tableau
  pl tableaux
tablespoonful
  pl tablespoonfuls
tablet
tabloid
taboo
tabor
tabulate
  tabulated
  tabulating
tacit
taciturn
taciturnity
tack
  pl tacks
  tin tacks: shoe tacks
tackle
  tackled

tackling

tacky

tact

tactful
  adv tactfully

tactical
  adv tactically

tactician

tactics

tactless

tadpole

taffeta

tag
  tagged
  tagging

tail
  a dog's tail:
  the tail of his coat:
  Did the police
  tail him?

tailed

tailing

tailor

tailored

tailoring

taint

take
  took
  He took a book
  taken
  He has taken a book
  taking

talc

talcum (powder)

tale
  a fairy tale

talent

talented

talisman

talk

talkative

tall

tallness

tallow

tally
  pl tallies
  tallied
  tallying

tally-ho

talon

tambourine

tame
  adv tamely
  tamed
  taming

tamper
  tampered
  tampering

tampon

tan
  tanned
  tanning

tandem

tang

tangent

tangerine

tangible
  adv tangibly

tangle
  tangled
  tangling

tango
  pl tangos

tank

tankard

tanker

tannery
  pl tanneries

tannin

tantalize, -ise
  tantalized
  tantalizing

tantamount to

tantrum

tap
  tapped
  The enemy tapped the
  telephone line: She
  tapped the table

  tapping

tape
  taped
  They taped the music
  taping

taper
  a lighted taper

  tapered
  tapering

tape recorder

tapestry
  pl tapestries

tapeworm

tapioca

tapir
  A tapir resembles
  a pig

tapped *see* tap

tar
  tarred
  tarring

tarantula

tardy
  adv tardily

tare
  Tare is the weight
  of an empty truck:
  weeds and tares

target
tariff
tarmac
tarmacadam
tarnish
tarpaulin
tarry
  tarried
  tarrying
tart
tartan
tartar
task
tassel
tasselled
taste
  tasted
  tasting
tasteful
  adv tastefully
tasteless
tasty
tattered
tatters
tattle
tattoo
  tattooed
  tattooing
taught *see* teach
taunt
taut
  The string is taut
tauten
  tautened
  tautening
tautological
  adv tautologically
tautology
tavern

208

tawdry
tawny
tax
  income tax
taxation
taxi
  pl taxis
  taxied
  taxiing
taxidermist
taxidermy
tea
  a cup of tea
teach
  taught
  She taught French
  teaching
teacher
teak
teal
team
  football team
team (up) with
  teamed (up) with
  teaming (up)
    with
teapot
tear [tēr]
  a tear of grief
tear [tār]
  to tear one's coat
tore
  She tore her coat
torn
  She has torn her coat
  tearing
tease
  teased
  teasing

teaser
teaspoonful
  pl teaspoonfuls
teat
technical
  adv technically
technicality
  pl technicalities
technician
technique
technological
  adv
    technologically
technologist
technology
  pl technologies
teddy-bear
tedious
tedium
tee
  *a golf tee: to tee
  a golf-ball*
teed
  teeing
teem
  *to teem with rain:
  to teem with fish*
  teemed
  teeming
teenage
teenager
teens
teeth *see* tooth
teethe
  *When do babies
  teethe?*
  teethed
  teething
teetotal

teetotaller
telegram
telegraph
telegraphic
telepathic
 adv telepathically
telepathy
telephone
 telephoned
 telephoning
telephonist
telephoto lens
telescope
 telescoped
 telescoping
telescopic
 adv telescopically
televise
 televised
 televising
television
tell
 told
 telling
teller
temerity
temper
 tempered
 tempering
temperament
temperamental
 adv temperamentally
temperance
temperate
temperature
tempest
tempestuous
temple

tempo
 pl tempos, tempi
temporal
 temporal,
 not spiritual
temporary
 a temporary job
temporize, -ise
 temporized
 temporizing
tempt
temptation
tempting
ten
tenable
tenacious
tenacity
tenancy
 pl tenancies
tenant
 tenanted
tend
tendency
 pl tendencies
tender
 tendered
 tendering
tendon
 a damaged tendon
 in his leg
tendril
tenet
tennis
tenon
 mortise and tenon
tenor
 a tenor and a soprano
tense
 adv tensely

tension
tent
tentacle
tentative
 adv tentatively
tenterhooks
tenth
tenuous
tenure
 land tenure
tepid
tercentenary
term
termagant
terminal
terminate
 terminated
 terminating
termination
terminology
terminus
 pl terminuses,
 termini
termite
tern
terrace
terracing
terracotta
terra firma
terrain
terrestrial
terrible
 adv **terribly**
terrier
terrific
 adv **terrifically**
terrify
 terrified
 terrifying

209

territorial
territory
  pl territories
terror
terrorism
terrorist
terrorize, -ise
  terrorized
  terrorizing
terse
  adv tersely
terseness
test
testament
testicle
testify
  testified
  testifying
testimonial
  Did her previous
  employer give her
  a testimonial?

testimony
  the testimony
  of the witness
  pl testimonies
testy
  adv testily
tetanus
tête-à-tête
tether
  tethered
  tethering
text
textile
textual
texture
than
thank

thankful
  adv thankfully
thankless
thanksgiving
that
thatch
  thatched
  thatching
thaw
the
theatre
theatrical
  adv theatrically
thee
theft
their
  They lost their gloves
theirs
them
theme
themselves
then
thence
theodolite
theologian
theological
theology
theorem
theoretic,
  theoretical
  adv theoretically
theorize, -ise
  theorized
  theorizing
theory
  pl theories
therapeutic
therapist
therapy

there
  There is no-one there:
  I saw it there
thereabouts
therefore
therm
thermal
Thermos ® (flask)
thermostat
thesaurus
these
thesis
  pl theses
they
they'd
  = they had, they
    would
they'll
  = they will
they're
  = they are
  They're coming today
thick
thicken
  thickened
  thickening
thicket
thickness
  pl thicknesses
thief
  pl thieves
thievish
thigh
thimble
thin
  compar thinner
  superl thinnest
  thinned
  thinning

thine
thing
think
  thought
  thinking
thinness
third
third-rate
thirst
thirsty
  adv thirstily
thirteen
thirteenth
thirtieth
thirty
this
thistle
thong
thorax
thorn
thorny
thorough
  a thorough search
thoroughfare
thoroughgoing
those
thou
though
thought
thought *see* think
thoughtful
  adv thoughtfully
thoughtfulness
thoughtless
thousand
thousandth
thrall
thrash
  Did he thrash that

child?: to thrash out
the problem

thread
threadbare
threadworn
threat
threaten
  threatened
  threatening
three
thresh
  to thresh corn
threshold
threw *see* throw
thrice
thrift
thrifty
  adv thriftily
thrill
thriller
thrilling
thrive
  thrived
  thriving
throat
throb
  throbbed
  throbbing
throes
  in the throes of moving
  house
thrombosis
throne
  the king's throne
throng
throttle
  throttled
  throttling
through

through the door
throughout
throw
  pl **throws**
  three throws
  of the dice
threw
  He threw a stone
thrown
  He has thrown a stone
throwing
thrush
  pl thrushes
thrust
  thrust
  thrusting
thud
  thudded
  thudding
thug
thumb
thump
thunder
  thundered
  thundering
thunderstruck
thundery
Thursday
thus
thwart
  thwarted
  thwarting
thy
thyme
  to season the sauce
  with thyme
thyroid
tiara
tic

a nervous tic

tick

*in a tick: a dog tick:
a tick at each answer:
the tick of a clock*

ticket

tickle
  tickled
  tickling

ticklish

tickly

tidal

tide

tidiness

tidings

tidy
  compar **tidier**
  superl **tidiest**
  adv **tidily**
  tidied
  tidying

tie
  tied
  tying

tier

*two tiers of the
wedding cake*

tiger

tigress
  pl **tigresses**

tight

tighten
  tightened
  tightening

tightness

tights

tile
  tiled
  He tiled the floor

tiling

till

tilled
  He tilled the land

tilling

tiller

tilt

timber
  The timber is rotting

timbre
  *the timbre of
  his voice*

time
  *What time is it?:
  to time a race*

  timed
  timing

timeless

timely

timetable

timid

timidity

timorous

timpani, tympani

tin
  tinned
  tinning

tincture

tinder

tinfoil

tinge
  tinged
  tinging

tingle
  tingled
  tingling

tinker
  tinkered
  tinkering

tinkle
  tinkled
  tinkling

tinsel

tint

tiny

tip
  tipped
  tipping

tipple

tipsy

tiptoe
  tiptoed
  tiptoeing

tirade

tire

*The runner began
to tire: Did the
journey tire you?*

  tired
  tiring

tireless

tiresome

tissue

tit

titbit

tithe

titivate
  titivated
  titivating

title
  titled

titter
  tittered
  tittering

tittle-tattle

titular

to
  to go to town

toad
toadstool
toady
  toadied
  toadying
toast
toaster
tobacco
tobacconist
toboggan
today
toddler
to-do
toe
  the toe of her shoe
toffee
together
togs
toil
  toiled
  toiling
toilet
token
told *see* tell
tolerable
  adv tolerably
tolerance
tolerate
  tolerated
  tolerating
toleration
toll
tomahawk
tomato
  pl **tomatoes**
tomb
  the tomb of the late king
tombola

tomboy
tombstone
tomcat
tome
  a learned Latin tome
tomfoolery
tomorrow
tomtom
ton
  a ton of coal
tone
  toned
  toning
tongs
tongue
tongue-tied
tonic
tonight
tonnage
tonne [tun]
  a tonne is a metric ton
**tonsilitis,
  tonsillitis**
tonsils
tonsure
too
  I am going too
took *see* take
tool
toot
  tooted
  tooting
tooth
  pl teeth
  She had two teeth filled
top
topaz

toper
topi, topee
  A topi is a sun-helmet
topiary
topic
topical
  adv topically
topmost
topography
topping
topple
  toppled
  toppling
topsyturvy
torch
  pl torches
tore *see* tear
torment
tormentor
torn *see* tear
tornado
  pl tornadoes
torpedo
  pl torpedoes
  torpedoed
  torpedoing
torpid
torpor
torrent
torrential
torrid
torso
  pl torsos
tortoise
tortoiseshell
tortuous
torture
  tortured
  torturing

Tory
pl Tories
toss
tot
total
  adv totally
totalled
  totalling
totalitarian
tote
totem pole
totter
  tottered
  tottering
tot up
  totted up
  totting up
touch
touchiness
touching
touchy
  adv touchily
tough
toughen
  toughened
  toughening
toupee
  toupees and wigs
tour
  toured
  touring
tourism
tourist
tournament
tourniquet
tousled
tout
  touted
  touting

tow
  to tow a car
  towed
  towing
toward
towards
towel
  towelled
  towelling
tower
  towered
  towering
town
toxic
toxin
toy
trace
  traced
  tracing
traceable
tracery
track
tract
traction
tractor
trade
  traded
  trading
trademark
trader
tradesman
trade union
trade unionist
tradition
traditional
  adv traditionally
traffic
  trafficked
  trafficking

tragedy
  pl tragedies
tragic
  adv **tragically**
trail
  trailed
  trailing
trailer
train
  trained
  training
trainee
trainer
trait
  Patience is not
  one of his traits
traitor
traitorous
tram
trammel
  trammelled
  trammelling
tramp
trample
  trampled
  trampling
trampoline
trance
tranquil
  adv tranquilly
tranquillity
tranquillizer, -iser
transaction
transatlantic
transcend
  transcended
  transcending
transcription
transept

transfer
transferred
transferring
transferable
transference
transfiguration
transfix
transform
transformation
transfuse
transfusion
transgression
transience
transient
transistor
transit
transition
transitional
transitive
transitory
  adv transitorily
translate
  translated
  translating
translation
translator
translucence
translucent
transmission
transmit
  transmitted
  transmitting
transmitter
transparency
  pl transparencies
transparent
transpire
  transpired
  transpiring

transplant
transport
transportation
transpose
  transposed
  transposing
  transposition
transverse
trap
  trapped
  trapping
trapeze
trapper
trappings
trash
trauma
traumatic
travel
  travelled
  travelling
  traveller
traverse
  traversed
  traversing
travesty
trawl
  trawled
  trawling
  trawler
tray
  cups and saucers
  on a tray
treacherous
treachery
treacle
tread
  trod
  He trod on her toe
  trodden

He has trodden on it
treadle
treason
treasonable
treasure
treasurer
treasury
  pl treasuries
treat
treatise
  a philosophical
  treatise
treatment
treaty
  pl treaties
  treaties signed
  after the war
treble
tree
trek
trellis
  pl trellises
tremble
  trembled
  trembling
tremendous
tremor
tremulous
trench
  pl trenches
trenchant
trencherman
trend
trendy
trepidation
trespass
  pl trespasses
tress
  pl tresses

trestle
trews
trial
triangle
triangular
tribal
tribe
tribulation
tribunal
tribune
tributary
  pl tributaries
tribute
trice
trick
trickery
trickle
  trickled
  trickling
trickster
tricky
tricolour
tricycle
trident
tried *see* try
triennial
tries *see* try
trifle
  trifled
  trifling
trifling
trigger
  triggered
  triggering
trigonometry
trill
trilogy
  pl trilogies
trim

trimmed
trimming
Trinity
trinket
trio
  pl trios
trip
  tripped
  tripping
tripe
triple
triplet
triplicate
tripod
tripper
trite
triumph
  triumphed
  triumphing
triumphal
triumphant
trivial
triviality
  pl trivialities
trod, trodden *see*
  tread
troll
trolley
  pl trolleys
trollop
trombone
troop
  a troop of soldiers:
  a cavalry troop: to
  troop out of the hall
  trooped
  trooping
  trooper
trophy

pl trophies
tropic
tropical
trot
  trotted
  trotting
  trotters
troubadour
trouble
  troubled
  troubling
troublesome
trough
trounce
  trounced
  trouncing
troupe
  a troupe of actors
trousers
trousseau
  pl trousseaux,
  trousseaus
trout
trowel
truancy
truant
truce
truck
truculent
trudge
  trudged
  trudging
true
truffle
truism
truly
trump
trumpet
truncated

truncheon
trundle
  trundled
  trundling
trunk
truss
  pl trusses
  trussed
  trussing
trust
trustee
trustful
  adv trustfully
trusting
trustworthy
trusty
truth
truthful
  adv truthfully
truthfulness
try
  pl tries
  tried
  trying
tryst
tsar, tzar, czar
tsetse
tub
tuba
tubby
tube
tuber
tuberculosis
tubing
tubular
tuck
Tuesday
tuft
tug

tugged
tugging
tug-of-war
tuition
tulip
tulle
tumble
  tumbled
  tumbling
tumbler
tumbrel, tumbril
tummy
  pl tummies
tumour
tumult
tumultuous
tun
  A tun is a large cask
tuna
tune
  tuned
  tuning
tuneful
  adv tunefully
tuneless
tunic
tunnel
  tunnelled
  tunnelling
turban
  He wore a turban
  on his head
turbine
  a turbine engine
turbot
turbulence
turbulent
tureen
turf

turgid
turkey
  pl turkeys
Turkish
turmoil
turn
turning
turnip
turnover
turnstile
turntable
turpentine
turquoise
turret
turreted
turtle
turtleneck
tusk
tussle
tutor
tutorial
tutu
twaddle
twang
tweak
tweed
tweezers
twelfth
twelve
twentieth
twenty
twice
twiddle
  twiddled
  twiddling
twig
twilight
twin
twine

217

twined
twining
twinge
twinkle
twinkled
twinkling
twirl
twist
twister
twitch
pl twitches
twitter
twittered
twittering
two
two apples
twofold
tycoon
a business tycoon
tympani *see*
timpani
type
typed
typing
typewriter
typhoid
typhoon
*The ship was sunk
in a typhoon*
typhus
typical
adv typically
typify
typified
typifying
typist
tyrannical
adv tyrannically
tyrannize, -ise

tyrannized
tyrannizing
tyrannous
tyranny
tyrant
tyre
a tyre for the car
tzar *see* tsar

U

ubiquitous
udder
ugliness
ugly
compar uglier
superl ugliest
ukelele, ukulele
ulcer
ulterior
ultimate
adv **ultimately**
ultimatum
pl ultimatums,
ultimata
ultrasonic
ultraviolet
umbilical
umbrage
umbrella
umpire
umpired
umpiring
unable
unaccountable
adv
unaccountably
unadulterated
unanimity

unanimous
unapproachable
unassuming
unaware
*I was unaware
of his presence*
unawares
*The blow took
him unawares*
unbalanced
unbend
unbent
unbending
unbridled
unburden
unburdened
unburdening
uncalled for
uncanniness
uncanny
adv uncannily
uncared for
uncertain
uncharted
uncle
uncoil
uncoiled
uncoiling
uncommon
uncompromising
unconscionable
*He has been an
unconscionable time
doing that job*

unconscious
*He was knocked
unconscious: He was
unconscious of the
trouble*

adv
unconsciously
uncouth
undaunted
undeniable
adv undeniably
under
undercarriage
underclothes
undercover
undercurrent
undercut
undercut
undercutting
underdeveloped
underdog
underdone
underestimate
underestimated
underestimating
underfoot
undergo
underwent
undergone
undergoing
undergraduate
underground
undergrowth
underhand
underline
underlined
underlining
underlying
undermine
undermined
undermining
underneath
underprivileged
underrate

underrated
underrating
undersigned
underskirt
understand
understood
understanding
understandable
adv
understandably
understate
understated
understating
understatement
understood *see*
understand
understudy
understudied
understudying
undertake
undertook
undertaken
undertaking
undertaker
undertone
undertook *see*
undertake
undervalue
undervalued
undervaluing
underwear
underwent *see*
undergo
underworld
underwrite
underwrote
underwritten
underwriting
underwriter

undo
undid
He undid his coat
undone
His coat is undone
undoing
undoubted
undress
undue
undulate
undulated
undulating
unduly
unearth
unearthly
uneasy
adv uneasily
unemployed
unemployment
unequal
unequalled
unequivocal
adv unequivocally
unerring
uneven
unexpected
unfailing
unfair
unfaithful
unfasten
unfastened
unfastening
unfit
unfitted
unflagging
unflinching
unfold
unforgettable
adv **unforgettably**

unfortunate
  adv **unfortunately**
unfounded
unfurl
ungainly
ungracious
ungrateful
  adv ungratefully
unguarded
unhappiness
unhappy
  adv unhappily
unhealthy
  adv unhealthily
unhinge
  unhinged
  unhinging
unicorn
unification
uniform
uniformity
unify
  unified
  unifying
uninterrupted
union
unique
  adv uniquely
unison
unit
unitary
unite
  united
  uniting
unity
universal
  adv universally
universe
university
220

pl universities
unkempt
unkind
unleash
unless
unlikely
unload
  unloaded
  unloading
unlooked for
unloose
  unloosed
  unloosing
unlucky
  adv unluckily
unmanly
unmask
unmentionable
unmistakable
  adv unmistakably
unmitigated
unmoved
unnecessary
  adv unnecessarily
unobtrusive
  adv unobtrusively
unpack
unpalatable
unparalleled
unpick
unpremeditated
unprepossessing
unpretentious
unprincipled
unravel
unravelled
unravelling
unremitting
unrequited

unrest
unrivalled
unruliness
unruly
unsavoury
unscathed
unscrew
unseasonable
unseen
unsettled
unsightly
unsophisticated
unsound
unspeakable
  adv unspeakably
unstudied
unsuspecting
unthinkable
until
untimely
unto
untold
untoward
untrue
untruth
untruthful
  adv untruthfully
unusual
  adv unusually
unvarnished
unveil
  unveiled
  unveiling
unwanted
  unwanted children
unwieldy
unwitting
unwonted
  = not usual

unwonted generosity
unworthy
up
upbraid
  upbraided
  upbraiding
upbringing
upgrade
  upgraded
  upgrading
upheaval
uphill
uphold
  upheld
  upholding
upholder
upholster
  upholstered
  upholstering
upholsterer
upholstery
upkeep
upland
upmost
upon
upper
uppermost
upright
uprising
uproar
uproarious
uproot
  uprooted
  uprooting
upset
  upset
  upsetting
upshot
upside-down

upstairs
upstanding
upstart
upstream
uptake
up-to-date
uranium
urban
  an urban motorway
urbane
  an urbane young man
urbanities
urchin
urge
  urged
  urging
urgency
urgent
urinary
urinate
  urinated
  urinating
urine
urn
us
usage
use
  used
  using
useful
  adv usefully
usefulness
useless
usher
  ushered
  ushering
usherette
usual
  adv **usually**

usurp
usurper
utensil
uterus
utility
  pl utilities
utilization, -isation
utilize, -ise
  utilized
  utilizing
utmost
utter
  uttered
  uttering
utterance
utterly

V

vacancy
  pl vacancies
vacant
vacate
  vacated
  vacating
vacation
  a summer vacation in Spain
vaccinate
  vaccinated
  vaccinating
vaccine
vacillate
  vacillated
  vacillating
vacuous
vacuum
vagabond
vagary

221

pl vagaries
vagina
vagrancy
vagrant
vague
  adv vaguely
vagueness
vain
  conceited and vain
valance
vale
  the Vale of Evesham
valency
  pl valencies
valentine
valet
valiant
valid
validity
valley
  pl valleys
valorous
valour
valuable
valuation
valuator
value
  valued
  valuing
valuer
valve
vamp
vampire
van
vandal
vandalism
vandalize, -ise
  vandalized
  vandalizing

vane
  a weather vane
vanguard
vanilla
vanish
vanity
  pl vanities
vanquish
vantage
vapid
vaporize, -ise
  vaporize
  vaporizing
vaporizer, -iser
vapour
variable
  adv variably
variance
variant
variation
varicose
varied
variegated
variety
  pl **varieties**
various
varnish
  pl varnishes
vary
  varied
  varying
vase
Vaseline®
vassal
vast
vat
vaudeville
vault
vaunt

veal
veer
  veered
  veering
vegetable
vegetarian
vegetate
  vegetated
  vegetating
vegetation
vehemence
vehement
vehicle
vehicular
veil
  a bride's veil:
  to veil in mystery
veiled
veiling
vein
  a clot of blood in
  a vein: a vein of
  cheerfulness
veined
vellum
velocity
  pl velocities
velvet
velveteen
velvety
venal
  corrupt and
  venal lawyers
vendetta
vending
vendor
veneer
venerable
venerate

venerated
venerating
veneration
venereal disease
Venetian blind
vengeance
vengeful
venial
venial sins
venison
venom
venomous
vent
ventilate
ventilated
ventilating
ventilation
ventilator
ventricle
ventriloquism
ventriloquist
venture
ventured
venturing
venue
veracity
*They doubted the
veracity of his
statement*
verandah,
veranda
verb
verbal
adv verbally
verbatim
verbose
verbosity
verdant
verdict

verdigris
verdure
verge
verged
verging
verger
verification
verify
verified
verifying
verily
veritable
adv veritably
vermicelli
vermilion
vermin
verminous
vermouth
vernacular
vernal
verruca
versatile
versatility
verse
version
versus
vertebra
pl vertebrae
vertebrate
vertex
the vertex of a cone
pl vertices
vertical
adv **vertically**
vertigo
verve
very
vespers
vessel

vest
vestibule
vestige
vestigial
vestry
pl vestries
vet
vetted
vetting
veteran
**veterinary
surgeon**
veto
pl vetoes
vetoed
vetoing
vex
vexed
vexing
vexation
vexatious
via
viable
viaduct
viands
vibrant
vibrate
vibrated
vibrating
vibration
vicar
vicarious
vice
viceroy
vice versa
vicinity
vicious
vicissitude
victim

victimization,
-isation
victimize, -ise
  victimized
  victimizing
victor
victorious
victory
  pl victories
victuals
videotape
vie
  vied
  vying
view
viewpoint
vigil
vigilance
vigilant
  to keep a vigilant watch
vigilante
  The viligantes helped the police
vignette
vigorous
vigour
Viking
vile
vilify
  vilified
  vilifying
villa
village
villager
villain
villainous
villainy
  pl villainies

vindicate
vindicated
vindicating
vindictive
  adv vindictively
vine
vinegar
vineyard
vintage
viola
violate
  violated
  violating
violation
violence
violent
violet
violin
violinist
violoncello
viper
virago
  pl viragos
virgin
virginal
virginity
virile
virility
virtual
  adv virtually
virtue
virtuosity
virtuoso
  pl virtuosos
virtuous
virulence
virulent
virus
  pl viruses

visa
  pl visas
visage
vis-à-vis
viscera
viscid
viscosity
viscount
viscountess
  pl viscountesses
viscous
visibility
visible
  adv visibly
vision
visionary
  pl visionaries
visit
  visited
  visiting
visitation
visitor
visor
vista
  pl vistas
visual
  adv visually
visualize, -ise
  visualized
  visualizing
vital
  adv vitally
vitality
vitamins
vitreous
vitrified
vitriol
vituperation
vituperative

vivacious
vivacity
viva voce
vivid
vividness
vivisection
vixen
viz
vizier
vocabulary
  pl vocabularies
vocal
  adv vocally
vocation
  a vocation to be
  a priest
vocational
vociferous
vodka
vogue
voice
  voiced
  voicing
void
volatile
volcanic
volcano
  pl volcanoes
vole
volition
volley
  pl volleys
volt
voltage
volubility
voluble
  adv volubly
volume
voluminous

voluntary
  adv voluntarily
volunteer
  volunteered
  volunteering
voluptuous
vomit
  vomited
  vomiting
voracious
voracity
  the voracity of
  his appetite
vortex
  the vortex of a
  whirlpool
  pl vortices,
    vortexes
vote
  voted
  voting
vouch
voucher
vow
  vowed
  vowing
vowel
voyage
  voyaged
  voyaging
vulgar
vulgarity
vulnerable
vulture

W

wad
wadding

waddle
  waddled
  waddling
wade
  waded
  wading
wader
wafer
  an ice cream wafer
waffle
  waffled
  waffling
waft
wag
  wagged
  The dog wagged
  his tail
  wagging
wage
  waged
  He waged war
  waging
wagged *see* wag
waggle
  waggled
  waggling
waggon
waif
  a poor little waif
wail
  wailed
  wailing
waist
  She has a tiny waist
wait
waiter
waiting-room
waitress
waive

225

*to waive the right
to the throne*

waived

waiving

wake

woke, waked

*He woke up in
the night*

woken, wakened

You've woken him

waking

wakeful

waken

wakened

wakening

walk

walkie-talkie

wall

wallaby

pl wallabies

wallet

wallop

walloped

walloping

wallow

wallpaper

walnut

walrus

pl walruses

waltz

pl waltzes

wan

wand

wander

wandered

wandering

wanderer

wanderlust

wane

waned

waning

wangle

wangled

wangling

want

*dying of want:
for want of money:
They want money*

wanton

war

warred

warring

warble

warbled

warbling

warbler

ward

warded

warding

warden

warden of the hostel

warder

a prison warder

wardrobe

ware

*earthenware,
stoneware*

warehouse

wares

*He sold his wares
at the fair*

warfare

wariness

warlike

warm

warmth

warn

warp

warpath

warrant

warren

warrior

warship

wart

wary

adv warily

was *see* be

wash

washer

wash-hand basin

wasp

wastage

waste

*a waste of food:
to waste food*

wasted

wasting

wasteful

adv wastefully

waster

wastrel

wastepaper
basket

watch

pl watches

watchful

adv watchfully

watchman

pl watchmen

water

watered

watering

waterfall

waterlogged

waterproof

watery

watt

wattage
wattle
wave

*He gave a friendly
wave: a heat wave:
Did he wave to you?*

waved
waving
wavelength
waver

to waver and hesitate

wavered
wavering
wavy
wax
waxy
way

*the way home: the
way she wears her
hair*

wayfarer
waylay
waylaid
waylaying
wayside
wayward
we
weak

a weak child

weaken
weakened
weakening
weakling
weakly

*a sick and
weakly child*

weakness
wealth
wealthy

compar **wealthier**
superl **wealthiest**
wean
weaned
weaning
weapon
wear

*She often wears
an apron*

wore

She wore the dress

worn

She's worn that before

wearing
wearable
wearer
wearisome
weary

adv **wearily**
wearied
wearying
weasel
weather
weathered
weathering
weatherbeaten
weathervane
weave
wove

She wove cloth

woven

She has woven a rug

weaving
weaver
web
webbed
webbing
wed
wedded

wedding
we'd

= we had, we
would

wedding
wedge
wedged
wedging
wedlock
Wednesday
weed
weedy
week

two days a week

weekday
weekend
weekly

*a weekly paper:
He visits his mother
weekly*

weep
wept
weeping
weigh

to weigh the potatoes

weighed
weighing
weight
weighty
weir
weird
welcome
welcomed
welcoming
weld
welder
welfare
well

compar **better**

superl best
we'll
= we shall, we
will
wellingtons
well-off
well-to-do
well up
welled up
welling up
Welsh rarebit
welt
welter
wench
pl wenches
wend
went *see* go
wept *see* weep
were *see* be
we're
= we are
weren't
= were not
werewolf
west
westerly
a westerly wind
western
western ideas
westward
westwards
wet
a wet day:
to wet the carpet
compar wetter
superl wettest
wet
wetting
wetness

we've
= we have
whack
whale
whaler
wharf
pl wharves,
wharfs
what
whatever
whatsoever
wheat
wheaten
wheedle
wheedled
wheedling
wheel
wheeled
wheeling
wheelbarrow
wheelchair
wheeze
wheezed
wheezing
whelk
whelp
when
whence
whenever
where
whereabouts
whereas
wherefore
whereupon
wherever
wherewithal
whet
to whet the appetite
whetted

whetting
whether
which
whichever
whiff
while
while away
whiled away
whiling away
whilst
whim
whimper
whimpered
whimpering
whimsical
adv whimsically
whimsy
pl whimsies
whine
whined
whining
whinny
pl whinnies
whinnied
whinnying
whip
whipped
whipping
whippet
whirl
whirr
whisker
whisky
pl whiskies
whisper
whispered
whispering
whist
whistle

whistled
whistling
whit
not a whit
white
whiten
whitened
whitening
whiteness
whitewash
whither
whiting
Whitsun, Whit
whittle
whittled
whittling
whizz
who
whoever
whole
a whole orange:
the whole household
adv **wholly**
wholesale
wholesome
who'll
= who will
whom
whoop
She gave a whoop
of joy: to whoop
with joy
whooped
whooping
whooping-cough
whore
the whore of Babylon
whose
why

wick
wicked
wickedness
wicker
wicket
wide
adv **widely**
widen
widened
widening
widespread
widow
widower
width
wield
wielded
wielding
wife
pl **wives**
wig
wiggle
wiggled
wiggling
wiggly
wigwam
wild
wilderness
wildness
wile
wilful
adv **wilfully**
will
would
I would go if I could
will
willed
She willed him to
win: He willed her
all his money

willing
will-o'-the-wisp
willow
willowy
willynilly
wilt
wily
win
won
winning
wince
winced
wincing
winch
pl **winches**
wind [wind]
winded
The blow winded him
winding
wind [wīnd]
wound
He wound the bandage
round her arm
winding
windfall
windmill
window
windscreen
windy
wine
wing
winged
wink
winkle
winnings
winsome
winter
wintered
wintering

wintry
wipe
  wiped
  wiping
wiper
wire
  wired
  wiring
wireless
wiry
wisdom
wise
  adv wisely
wish
  pl wishes
wishbone
wishful
wishywashy
wisp
wistful
  adv wistfully
wistfulness
wit
  cleverness and wit
witch
  pl witches
witchcraft
with
withdraw
  withdrew
  He withdrew his application
  withdrawn
  He has withdrawn his application
  withdrawing
withdrawal
wither
  withered

withering
withhold
  withheld
  withholding
within
without
withstand
  withstood
  withstanding
witness
  pl witnesses
witticism
wittingly
  He did not wittingly deceive her
witty
  adv wittily
  He spoke wittily and interestingly
wizard
wizened
wobble
  wobbled
  wobbling
wobbly
woe
  sadness and woe
woebegone
woeful
  adv woefully
woke, woken *see* wake
wolf
  pl wolves
  wolfed
  wolfing
wolfish
woman
  pl women

womanhood
womanly
womb
won *see* win
wonder
  wondered
  wondering
wonderful
  adv wonderfully
wonderland
wonderment
wondrous
wont
  as he was wont to do
won't
  = will not
woo
  to woo a girl and marry her
  wooed
  He wooed her ardently
  wooing
wood
  a beech wood: wood for the fire
  wooded
wooden
woodland
woodpecker
woodwork
woody
wooed *see* woo
wooer
wool
woollen
woolly
word
wording
wordy

wore *see* wear
work
workable
worker
workman
  pl workmen
workmanship
world
worldly
worm
worn *see* wear
worry
  pl worries
  worried
  worrying
worse
worsen
  worsened
  worsening
worship
  worshipped
  worshipping
worshipful
  adv worshipfully
worst
worsted
worth
worthless
worthy
  adv worthily
would *see* will
would-be
wound [wōōnd]
  a bullet wound
wound [wownd]
  see wind
wove, woven *see*
  weave
wraith

wrangle
  wrangled
  wrangling
wrap
  to wrap in paper
  wrapped
  *The book was wrapped
  in brown paper*
  wrapping
wrapper
wrath
wrathful
  adv **wrathfully**
wreak
  *to wreak vengeance:
  to wreak havoc*
  wreaked
  wreaking
wreath
  a wreath of flowers
wreathe
  *to wreathe in flowers:
  to wreathe in smiles*
  wreathed
  wreathing
wreck
  *a wreck on the
  sea-bed: to wreck
  the car*
  wrecked
  wrecking
wreckage
wren
wrench
  pl wrenches
wrest
  *to wrest it from
  his grasp*
wrestle

wrestled
wrestling
wrestler
wrestling
wretch
  a poor wretch
  pl wretches
wretched
wriggle
  wriggled
  wriggling
wring
  *to wring the clothes:
  to wring a promise
  from her*
wrung
  She wrung the clothes
wringing
wringer
wrinkle
  wrinkled
  wrinkling
wrist
writ
write
  to write neatly
wrote
  He wrote a letter
written
  *He has written
  a letter*
writing
writhe
  writhed
  writhing
wrong
wrongdoer
wrongful
  adv **wrongfully**

wrote *see* write
wrought-iron
wrung *see* wring
wry
  a wry smile:
  a wry neck

X

X-ray
  X-rayed
  X-raying
xenophobia
xenophobic
Xerox®
xylophone

Y

yacht
yachting
yachtsman
yak
yank
yap
  yapped
  yapping
yard
yardstick
yarn
yashmak
yawn
year
yearling
yearly
yearn
yeast

yell
yellow
yelp
yen
yeoman
yes
yesterday
yet
Yeti
yew
  a yew tree
yield
yodel
  yodelled
  yodelling
yoga
yoghourt
yoke
  the yoke of a plough:
  the yoke of a dress
yokel
yolk
  the yolk of an egg
yonder
yore
  days of yore
you
  you and I
you'd
  = you had, you
    would
you'll
  = you will
young
youngster
your
  your house
you're
  = you are

yourselves
youth
youthful
  adv youthfully
you've
  = you have
Yo-Yo®
Yule

Z

zany
zeal
zealot
zealous
zebra
zenith
zephyr
zero
zest
zestful
  adv zestfully
zigzag
  zigzagged
  zigzagging
zinc
zip
  zipped
  zipping
zither
zodiac
zone
zoo
zoological
zoologist
zoology
zoom
  zoomed
  zooming

Words liable to be confused

a
an

aboard
abroad

accept
except

access
excess

acme
acne

ad
add

adapter
adaptor

addition
edition

adverse
averse

advice
advise

aesthetic
ascetic

affect
effect

affluent
effluent

ail
ale

air
heir

aisle
isle

ale
ail

all
awl

allay
alley

allegory
allergy

alley
allay

alliterate
illiterate

allude
elude

allusion
delusion
illusion

altar
alter

alteration
altercation

alternately
alternatively

amateur
amateurish

amend
emend

amiable
amicable

among
between

amoral
immoral
immortal

an
a

angel
angle

annals
annuals

annex
annexe

annuals
annals

ant
aunt

antiquated
antique

arc
ark

arisen
arose

arose
arisen

artist
artiste

ascent
assent

ascetic
aesthetic

assay
essay

assent
ascent

astrology
astronomy

ate
eaten

aunt
ant

aural
oral

averse
adverse

awl
all

axes
axis

bad
bade

bade
bid

bail
bale
bale out

baited
bated

bale
bale out
bail

ball
bawl

ballet
ballot

banns
bans

bare
bear

barn
baron
barren

base
bass

bass (pl)
basses

bated
baited

bath
bathe

baton
batten

bawl
ball

bazaar
bizarre

be
bee

beach
beech

bean
been
being

bear
bare

beat
beaten

beat
beet

beau
bow

became
become

bee
be

beech
beach

been
bean

being

beer
bier

beet
beat

befallen
befell

began
begun

being

bean
been

belief
believe

bell
belle

bellow
below

beret
berry
bury

berth
birth

beside
besides

between
among

bid
bade

bier
beer

bight
bite

birth
berth

bit
bitten

bite
bight

bizarre
bazaar

blew
blown

blew
blue

bloc
block

blond
blonde

blown
blew

blue
blew

boar
boor
bore

board
bored

boast
boost

bonny
bony

bookie
bouquet

boor
boar
bore

boost
boast

bootee
booty

bore
boar
boor

bore
born
borne

borough
burgh

bough
bow

bound
bounded

bouquet
bookie

bow
beau

bow
bough

boy
buoy

brae
bray

brake
break

234

brassière
brazier

bray
brae

brazier
brassière

breach
breech

bread
bred

break
brake

breath
breathe

bred
bread

breech
breach

bridal
bridle

broach
brooch

broke
broken

brooch
broach

buffet
['buffit]
buffet
['boŏfā]

buoy
boy

burgh
borough

bury
beret
berry

but
butt

buy
by
bye

cache
cash

caddie
caddy

calf
calve

callous
callus

calve
calf

came
come

canned
could

cannon
canon

can't
cant

canvas
canvass

carat
carrot

cart
kart

cartilage
cartridge

carton
cartoon

cartridge
cartilage

cash
cache

cast
caste

cavalier
cavalry

ceiling
sealing

cell
sell

cellular
cellulose

censor
censure

cent
scent
sent

centenarian
centenary

cereal
serial

chafe
chaff

charted
chartered

chased
chaste

cheap
cheep

check
cheque

checked
chequered

cheep
cheap

cheque
check

chilli
chilly

choir
quire

choose
chose
chosen

chord
cord

chose
choose
chosen

chute
shoot

cite
sight
site

clothes
cloths

coarse
course

collage
college

coma
comma

come
came

comma
coma

commissionaire
commissioner

complement
compliment

complementary
complimentary

concert
consort

confidant
confidante
confident

235

conscience
conscientious
conscious

consort
concert

consul
council
counsel

continual
continuous

coop
coup

coral
corral

cord
chord

co-respondent
correspondent

cornet
coronet

cornflour
cornflower

coronet
cornet

corps
corpse

corral
coral

correspondent
co-respondent

cost
costed

could
canned

council
counsel
consul

councillor
counsellor

coup
coop

course
coarse

courtesy
curtsy

creak
creek

crevasse
crevice

crochet
crotchet

cue
queue

curb
kerb

currant
current

curtsy
courtesy

cygnet
signet

cymbal
symbol

dairy
diary

dam
damn

dammed
damned

damn
dam

dear
deer

decry
descry

deer
dear

delusion
allusion
illusion

dependant
dependent

deprecate
depreciate

descendant
descendent

descry
decry

desert
dessert

device
devise

devolution
evolution

dew
due
Jew

diary
dairy

did
done

die
dye

died
dyed

dinghy
dingy

disbelief
disbelieve

discus
discuss

doe
dough

doily
dolly

done
did

dough
doe

draft
draught

dragon
dragoon

draught
draft

drawn
drew

drank
drunk

drew
drawn

driven
drove

drunk
drank

dual
duel

ducks
dux

dudgeon
dungeon

due
dew
Jew

duel
dual

dully
duly

dungeon
dudgeon

dux
ducks

dye
die

dyed
died

dyeing
dying

earthly
earthy

easterly
eastern

eaten
ate

eclipse
ellipse

economic
economical

edition
addition

eerie
eyrie

effect
affect

effluent
affluent

elder
eldest

elicit
illicit

eligible
legible

ellipse
eclipse

elude
allude

emend
amend

emigrant
immigrant

emigration
immigration

emission
omission

emphasis
emphasize

employee
employer

ensure
insure

entomologist
etymologist

envelop
envelope

epigram
epitaph
epithet

ere
err

erotic
erratic

err
ere

erratic
erotic

escapement
escarpment

essay
assay

etymologist
entomologist

evolution
devolution

ewe
yew
you

except
accept

excess
access

executioner
executor

exercise
exorcise

expand
expend

expansive
expensive

expatiate
expiate

expend
expand

expensive
expansive

expiate
expatiate

extant
extinct

eyrie
eerie

faerie
fairy

fain
feign

faint
feint

fair
fare

fairy
faerie

fallen
fell
felled

fare
fair

fate
fête

faun
fawn

feat
feet

feign
fain

feint
faint

fell
fallen
felled

ferment
foment

fête
fate

fiancé
fiancée

filed
filled

final
finale

fir
fur

fission
fissure

237

flair
flare

flammable
inflammable

flare
flair

flea
flee

flew
flu
flue

flew
flown

flocks
phlox

floe
flow

flour
flower

floury
flowery

flow
floe

flower
flour

flowery
floury

flown
flew

flu
flue
flew

foment
ferment

tont
fount

forbade
forbidden

fore
four

foregone
forgone

foresaw
foreseen

foreword
forward

forgave
forgiven

forgone
foregone

forgone
forwent

forgot
forgotten

forsaken
forsook

forswore
forsworn

fort
forte
forty

forth
fourth

forty
fort
forte

forward
foreword

forwent
forgone

foul
fowl

found
founded

fount
font

four
fore

fourth
forth

fowl
foul

franc
frank

freeze
frieze

froze
frozen

funeral
funereal

fur
fir

gabble
gable

gaff
gaffe

gait
gate

galleon
gallon

gamble
gambol

gaol
goal

gate
gait

gave
given

genie
genius
genus

genteel
gentile
gentle

genus
genie
genius

gild
guild

gilt
guilt

given
gave

glacier
glazier

goal
gaol

gone
went

gorilla
guerrilla

gourmand
gourmet

gradation
graduation

grate
great

grew
grown

grief
grieve

grill
grille

griped
gripped

grisly
gristly
grizzly

grope
group

ground
grounded

grown
grew

guerrilla
gorilla

guild
gild

guilt
gilt

hail
hale

hair
hare

half
halve

hallo
hallow
halo

halve
half

hangar
hanger

hanged
hung

hanger
hangar

hare
hair

hart
heart

heal
heel

hear
here

heart
hart

heel
heal

heir
air

here
hear

heron
herring

hew
hue

hewed
hewn

hid
hidden

higher
hire

him
hymn

hire
higher

hoar
whore

hoard
horde

hoarse
horse

hole
whole

honorary
honourable

hoop
whoop

hoped
hopped

horde
hoard

horse
hoarse

hue
hew

human
humane

humiliation
humility

hung
hanged

hymn
him

idle
idol

illegible
ineligible

illicit
elicit

illiterate
alliterate

illusion
allusion
delusion

immigrant
emigrant

immigration
emigration

immoral
amoral
immortal

immorality
immortality

impetuous
impetus

impracticable
impractical

in
inn

inapt
inept

incredible
incredulous

indigenous
indigent

industrial
industrious

ineligible
illegible

inept
inapt

inflammable
flammable

ingenious
ingenuous

inhuman
inhumane

inn
in

insure
ensure

intelligent
intelligible

interment
internment

invertebrate
inveterate

isle	knot	leak	llama
aisle	not	leek	lama
it's	knotty	led	load
its	naughty	lead	lode
jam	know	lee	loan
jamb	no	lea	lone
Jew	known	leek	loath
dew	knew	leak	loathe
due			
	lade	legible	local
jib	laid	eligible	locale
jibe	lay	lemming	lode
judicial	lied	lemon	load
judicious	lain	leopard	lone
junction	lane	leper	loan
juncture	lair	lessen	looped
kart	layer	lesson	loped
cart	lama	liable	lopped
kerb	llama	libel	loose
curb	lane	liar	lose
key	lain	lyre	loot
quay	laterally	libel	lute
knave	latterly	liable	loped
nave	lath	licence	lopped
knead	lathe	license	looped
kneed	latterly	lied	lose
need	laterally	lade	loose
knew	lay	laid	loth
known	lade	lay	loathe
knew	laid	lightening	lumbar
new	lied	lightning	lumber
knight	layer	lineament	lute
night	lair	liniment	loot
knightly	lea	liqueur	lyre
nightly	lee	liquor	liar
knit	lead	literal	macaroni
nit	led	literary	macaroon
		literate	

240

made	mayor	missal	mussel
maid	mare	missile	muscle
magnate	maze	mistaken	mystic
magnet	maize	mistook	mystique
maid	mean	mite	naught
made	mien	might	nought
mail	meat	moat	naughty
male	meet	mote	knotty
	mete out		
main		modal	naval
mane	medal	model	navel
	meddle	module	
maize			nave
maze	mediate	momentary	knave
	meditate	momentous	
male		momentum	navel
mail	meet		naval
	meat	moose	
mane	mete out	mouse	navvy
main		mousse	navy
	merino		
maniac	marina	moped	nay
manic		mopped	née
	metal		neigh
manner	mettle	moral	
manor		morale	need
	mete out		knead
mare	meat	morality	kneed
mayor	meet	mortality	
			negligent
marina	meter	mote	negligible
merino	metre	moat	
			neigh
marshal	mettle	motif	nay
martial	metal	motive	née
marten	mews	mouse	net
martin	muse	moose	nett
		mousse	
martial	mien		new
marshal	mean	mucous	knew
		mucus	
martin	might		night
marten	mite	multiple	knight
		multiply	
mask	miner		nightly
masque	minor	muscle	knightly
		mussel	
mat	minister		nit
matt	minster	muse	knit
		mews	

241

no	overthrew	peak	piazza
know	overthrown	peek	pizza
northerly	packed	pique	piece
northern	pact	peal	peace
not	pail	peel	pier
knot	pale	pear	peer
nougat	pain	pair	pined
nugget	pane	pare	pinned
nought	pair	pearl	piped
naught	pare	purl	pipped
nugget	pear	peasant	pique
nougat	palate	pheasant	peak
oar	palette	pedal	peek
ore	pallet	peddle	pistil
of	pale	peek	pistol
off	pail	peak	pizza
official	palette	pique	piazza
officious	palate	peel	place
omission	pallet	peal	plaice
emission	pane	peer	plain
oral	pain	pier	plane
aural	par	pence	plaintiff
ore	parr	pennies	plaintive
oar	pare	pendant	plait
organism	pear	pendent	plate
orgasm	pair	pennies	plane
outdid	parr	pence	plain
outdone	par	perquisite	plate
overcame	passed	prerequisite	plait
overcome	past	personal	plum
overdid	pastel	personnel	plumb
overdone	pastille	petrel	politic
overran	pate	petrol	political
overrun	pâté	pheasant	pool
overtaken	patty	peasant	pull
overtook	peace	phlox	poplar
	piece	flocks	popular

pore	proceed	quite	real
pour	precede	quiet	reel
pored	profit	racket	red
poured	prophet	racquet	read
poser	program	radar	reed
poseur	programme	raider	read
pour	proof	raged	reel
pore	prove	ragged	real
poured	property	raider	refuge
pored	propriety	radar	refugee
practicable	prophecy	rain	regal
practical	prophesy	reign	regale
practice	prophet	rein	reign
practise	profit	raise	rain
pray	propriety	raze	rein
prey	property	rampant	relief
precede	prostate	rampart	relieve
proceed	prostrate	ran	reproof
premier	prove	run	reprove
première	proof	rang	respectful
prerequisite	pull	ringed	respective
perquisite	pool	rung	rest
prey	purl	rap	wrest
pray	pearl	wrap	retch
price	put	raped	wretch
prise	putt	rapped	review
prize	quash	rapped	revue
principal	squash	rapt	rhyme
principle	quay	wrapped	rime
prise	key	rated	ridden
price	queue	ratted	rode
prize	cue	raze	right
private	quiet	raise	rite
privet	quite	read	write
prize	quire	red	rime
prise	choir	read	rhyme
price		reed	

243

ring	rye	sear	sewer
wring	wry	seer	sower
		sere	
ringed	sail		sewn
rang	sale	secret	sewed
rung		secrete	
	salon		sewn
risen	saloon	see	sown
rose		sea	
	sang		sextant
rite	sung	seem	sexton
right		seam	
write	sank		shaken
	sunk	seen	shook
road	sunken	saw	
rode			shear
rowed	saviour	seen	sheer
	savour	scene	
rode			sheared
ridden	saw	seer	sheered
	seen	sear	
roe		sere	shorn
row	sawed		shelf
	sawn	sell	shelve
rôle		cell	
roll	scared		shoe
	scarred	sensual	shoo
rose		sensuous	
risen	scene		shook
	seen	sent	shaken
rote		cent	
wrote	scent	scent	shoot
	cent		chute
rough	sent	septic	
ruff		sceptic	shorn
	sceptic		sheared
rout	septic	sere	sheered
route		sear	
	scraped	seer	showed
row	scrapped		shown
roe		serial	
	sculptor	cereal	shrank
rowed	sculpture		shrunk
road		series	
rode	sea	serious	sight
	see		cite
ruff		sew	site
rough	scaling	so	
	ceiling	sow	signet
run			cygnet
ran	seam	sewed	
	seem	sewn	silicon
rung			silicone
wrung			

244

singeing
singing

sinuous
sinus

site
cite
sight

skies
skis

slain
slew

slated
slatted

slay
sleigh

slew
slain

sloe
slow

sloped
slopped

slow
sloe

smelled
smelt

sniped
snipped

so
sew
sow

soar
sore

sociable
social

solder
soldier

sole
soul

some
sum

son
sun

soot
suit

sore
soar

soul
sole

southerly
southern

sow
sew
so

sowed
sown

sower
sewer

sown
sewn

spared
sparred

speciality
specialty

species
specious

sped
speeded

spoke
spoken

sprang
sprung

squash
quash

staid
stayed

stair
stare

stake
steak

stalk
stock

stanch
staunch

stank
stunk

stare
stair

stared
starred

stationary
stationery

statue
statute

staunch
stanch

stayed
staid

steak
stake

steal
steel

step
steppe

stile
style

stimulant
stimulus

stock
stalk

stocked
stoked

storey
story

straight
strait

straightened
straitened

stratum
stratus

strewed
strewn

strife
strive

striped
stripped

strive
strife

striven
strove

stunk
stank

sty
stye

style
stile

suede
swede

suit
soot

suite
sweet

sum
some

summary
summery

sun
son

sundae
Sunday

sung
sang

sunk
sank
sunken

super
supper

surplice
surplus

swam
swum

swede
suede

sweet
suite

swelled
swollen

swingeing
swinging

swollen
swelled

swore
sworn

swum
swam

symbol
cymbal

tacks
tax

tail
tale

taken
took

tale
tail

taped
tapped

taper
tapir

tapped
taped

tare
tear

taught
taut

tax
tacks

tea
tee

team
teem

tear
tare

tear

tier
tee

tea
teem

team
teeth
teethe

temporal
temporary

tendon
tenon

tenor
tenure

testimonial
testimony

their
there
they're

thorough
through

thrash
thresh

threw
through

threw
thrown

throes
throws

throne
thrown

through
thorough

through
threw

thrown
threw

thrown
throne

throws
throes

thyme
time

tic
tick

tier
tear

tiled
tilled

timber
timbre

time
thyme

tire
tyre

to
too
two

toe
tow

tomb
tome

ton
tonne
tun

too
to
two

took
taken

topi
toupee

tore
torn

tow
toe

trait
tray

treaties
treatise

trod
trodden

troop
troupe

tun
ton
tonne

turban
turbine

two	vortex	westerly	would
to	vertex	western	wood
too		wet	wooed
tycoon	wafer	whet	
typhoon	waver		wove
	waged	whit	woven
tyre	wagged	wit	
tire			wrap
	waif	whole	rap
unaware	waive	hole	
unawares	wave		wrapped
		whoop	rapped
unconscionable	waist	hoop	rapt
unconscious	waste		
		whore	wreak
undid	want	hoar	wreck
undone	wont		
		willed	wreath
unwanted	warden	would	wreathe
unwonted	warder		
		winded	wrest
urban	ware	wound	rest
urbane	wear		
		wit	wretch
vacation	waste	whit	retch
vocation	waist		
		withdrawn	wring
vain	wave	withdrew	ring
vane	waif		
vein	waive	wittily	write
		wittingly	right
vale	waver		rite
veil	wafer	woe	
		woo	wrote
venal	way		rote
venial	weigh	woke	
		woken	wrote
veracity	weak		written
voracity	week	wont	
		want	wrung
vertex	wear		rung
vortex	ware	woo	
		woe	wry
vigilant	weekly		rye
vigilante	weakly	wore	
		worn	yew
vocation	weigh		ewe
vacation	way	would	you
		willed	
voracity	went		yoke
veracity	gone		yolk
			yore
			your